# THE LITTLE
# DOS 6
## BOOK

*Kay Yarborough Nelson*

Peachpit Press
Berkeley, California

**THE LITTLE DOS 6 BOOK**
Kay Yarborough Nelson

Peachpit Press, Inc.
2414 Sixth St.
Berkeley, CA 94710
(510) 548-4393
(510) 548-5991 (fax)

**Notice of Liability**
The information in this book is distributed on an "As is"
basis, without warranty. While every precaution has been
taken in the preparation of this book, neither the author
nor Peachpit Press, Inc., shall have any liability to any person
or entity with respect to any liability, loss, or damage caused
or alleged to be caused directly or indirectly by the instructions contained in this book or by the computer software
and hardware products described herein.

**Trademarks**
Throughout this book, trademarked names are used. Rather
than put a trademark symbol in every occurrence of a trademarked name, we are using the names only in an editorial
fashion and to the benefit of the trademark owner, with no
intention of infringement of the trademark.

ISBN 0-56609-056-3

0 9 8 7 6 5 4 3 2 1

Printed and bound in the United States of America

# Contents

# Introduction

DOS—your computer's disk operating system—has some pretty impressive capabilities, but most of us don't need to know everything there is to know about them. All we do is day-to-day chores such as formatting disks, copying files and disks, deleting and renaming files, and things like that. And that's what this book concentrates on: helping you do those daily jobs and giving you some tips you can use to speed them up or straighten them out. You can also grab this book when you get stuck and don't know what to do next; it won't take up much room on your desk.

If you've never used a computer before, you'll find an introduction to some of its mysteries in Chapter 1 (like where the power switch is and which disk drive is which). You can skip that chapter if you know all that already. Chapter 2 will give you a guided tour of DOS's graphic interface, called the Shell, so that you can get an idea of how to use it and what it can do. Then the book will discuss, in short chapters, the kinds of skills and topics you need to know more about so that you can actually do productive work with your computer without having to read some fat book that was really written for programmers.

This book assumes that you'll want to use the Shell for the things that are easiest to do with the Shell. For example, you can rename directories with the Shell; you can't do that at the command line! You can also start a program by double-clicking on it. And you can type the first few characters of a file's name to immediately go to it. Some things you can't do in the Shell, though, and you have to use the command line (or the Run command). You can look up all the DOS commands, complete with everyday examples of how you'd use them, in the back of the book.

## Why DOS 6?

There are lots of reasons to switch to DOS 6. First, DOS 6 will make it much easier to manage your memory. If you're running Microsoft Windows, you'll appreciate the new MEM-MAKER command that optimizes memory. Windows is a memory hog and wants as much as it can get for itself (and its programs). If you're not running Windows, DOS 6 will give you a lot of the same features that Windows does, even if your computer is an old XT clone. You can run several programs at once and switch between them by using the Shell's graphical interface. You just won't be able to cut and paste between programs like you can in Windows.

Second, DOS 6 comes with a built-in disk compression program that can really free up room on your disks. The results can be quite dramatic. I went from 3 Mb of free space to 85 Mb of free space on a 200-Mb hard disk! And the Double-Space utility is really easy to use.

Third, there are all sorts of neat new utilities—including one that finally turns Num Lock off! If you've ever been bothered by having the Num Lock key on, you'll appreciate this one. There's also a built-in anti-virus programs as well as a sophisticated MSBACKUP utility that thankfully replaces the old BACKUP and RESTORE commands (who used them, anyway?) UNDELETE is more reliable and easier to use, too. And these utilities come in both DOS and Windows versions.

The installation program for DOS 6 has been simplified. New commands have been added, such as MOVE, which finally lets you move files and directories, and DELTREE, which lets you instantly delete directories and subdirectories full of files. New POWER and INTERLNK commands simplify using notebook computers, MSD analyzes your system without your having to take your computer apart, and Help has been vastly improved to actually show you examples of how to use commands. These are just a few of the most spectacular features; there are more that operate behind the scenes to make working with DOS easier and let advanced users create startups screens, troubleshoot DOS on startup, optimize disks, and more.

Try it; you'll like it.

## Acknowledgments

Many thanks to Peter Ivey for redesigning and laying out this edition of *The Little DOS Book* in Quark XPress. Headings are PMN Caecilia and text is Plantin, both from Adobe. Screen shots were taken with HiJaak from Inset Systems and Collage Plus from Inner Media, Inc.

**"Pay no attention to the little man behind the curtain!"** —FRANK MORGAN as the Wizard in MGM's *The Wizard of Oz* (1939)

# DOS: The Basic Basics

DOS is your computer's operating system. Without it, your computer and your favorite programs, like Lotus 1-2-3, Word-Perfect, and even Windows wouldn't run. DOS, which stands for Disk Operating System, is the little man behind the curtain, controlling everything. And unfortunately, we're not in Oz, and you do have to pay some attention to it. Some, but hopefully not a lot.

If DOS isn't already on your computer, you'll need to install it. How can you tell whether it's there or not? Turn on your computer. The ON switch is probably on the right side or on the front. It's usually red. You may also need to switch on the power to your monitor, or video screen. That control is normally under the front edge of the monitor.

## The Command Line

OK, does the computer start (it may take a minute to start up, or "boot") and do you see an A> or C>? Or something that begins with A:\> or C:\> or maybe even D:\>? That's called the **DOS prompt,** and it indicates that DOS is waiting for you to type a command there (that's why it's also called the **command line**). If you see the C:\> (or one of the variations),

DOS is there. Check to see what version it is by typing *ver* and pressing Enter (that funny-looking key on the right side of the keyboard; it may just be labeled with a bent arrow on it). If you're not running version 6 (or if you're not running DOS at all), go to the appendix, which will tell you how to install DOS 6.

**TIP**— *You can use DOS either with the Shell or with the command line.*

You may instead see a screen like this one when your computer starts.

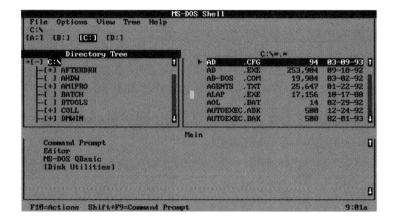

This is called the **Shell**. DOS may have been set up to show you this screen when it was installed. If it doesn't come up automatically, and you want it to, see Chapter 10 for how to set things up that way.

**TIP**— *To switch from the Shell to the command line, press Shift-F9. To switch back from the command line to the Shell, type* exit *and press Enter.*

The Shell lets you pick and choose from menus instead of having to remember the special commands for everything you do, so it's a lot easier to use than giving DOS direct commands.

To see the Shell if it's not showing, type *dosshell* at the DOS prompt and press Enter.

As you can tell from its name, DOS 6 is the latest in a long series of DOS's. What's the difference? Well, anything earlier than version 3.3 is pretty useless if you've got a hard disk, and you probably do. Version 3.3 was designed to handle large hard disks, whereas the earlier versions of DOS weren't. Version 4 added a shell feature, but it took up so much memory that a lot of people didn't want to use it. The Shell was improved beginning with DOS 5 to take up less memory and also give you more features, like being able to switch between programs quickly, get online help, get files and directories back if you accidentally erase them, search for the particular file you're looking for, and unformat disks and do quick formats. In fact, the Shell is quite similar to Microsoft Windows. It gives you a graphical interface with icons (small pictorial representations of what you see on the screen) and menus that you can use with or without a mouse. You can also have several programs running and switch between them by pressing a "hot key." You'll take a guided tour of the Shell in the next chapter so that you can get an idea of what it can do. But first, you need some basic skills so that you can "talk" to DOS.

# The Keyboard

Because a lot of what you do with DOS is done with the keyboard, let's take a quick look at some of those funny keys.

## The Enter Key

The most important one is the **Enter key**. As you saw earlier, it's the weird-looking key on the right side of your keyboard. It's probably gray. It may be labeled Return. We'll call it the Enter key because you use it to *enter* commands. DOS can't read what you've typed until you press Enter.

## The Backspace Key

The second most important key is the **Backspace key**. It's just above the Enter key, and it has a backward-pointing arrow on it. It may or may not be labeled Backspace, but that's what it is. You use it to correct mistakes. When you press Backspace, you erase the character to the left of the cursor (the blinking underline). So if you make a mistake in typing

**TIP—** *You can also delete text with the Del key.*

before you press Enter, just press Backspace, erase it, and correct it. You'll see more about entering commands later in the book.

## The Function Keys

The gray keys labeled F1 through F10 (you may have more than those, depending on what keyboard you have) are either on the left side of the keyboard or across the top.

**Tip**— *If you see an instruction to use the F1 key, press the gray F1 key; don't type f and 1.*

## The Numeric Keypad

Over on the far-right side of your keyboard is an arrangement of number keys that may also have arrows on them. That's the **numeric keypad**. It's designed to be used to enter numbers quickly, like a ten-key calculator. When Num Lock is on (you toggle it on and off by pressing the Num Lock key) and you press those number keys, you get numbers. When Num Lock's off, those keys move the cursor. You may have a light on your keyboard that comes on when Num Lock is on, or you may not. On some keyboards, Num Lock comes on when you start your computer.

You'll also see Home and End on a couple of these keys. You can use them to go to the beginning and end of a list. The keys marked PgUp and PgDn also move you through lists, one screen at a time.

## The Cursor Keys

If you have an older keyboard, you'll need to use the numeric keypad (with Num Lock off) to move the cursor. Look closely, and you'll see arrows on the 4, 8, 6, and 2 keys. They represent the direction the cursor will go when you press that key. To move the cursor down one line, you'd press 2, and so forth.

**Tip**— *The cursor isn't the same as the prompt. The cursor is a small blinking underline that shows you where you are on a line.*

If you've got a newer keyboard, there'll be **cursor keys** at the bottom of the keyboard on the right. They're arranged in an upside-down T formation. They'll move the cursor so that you don't have to worry about whether Num Lock is on or not.

## Other Keys

There are a lot of other keys, aren't there? Here are a few more you may need to know about:

- The **Esc key**, on the upper-left side of the keyboard, will cancel a command.

- The **Tab key**, just under the Esc key, moves the cursor one tab space. You also use it to move from area to area in the Shell. It may not be marked Tab but may have two arrows on it, or it may have Tab and the two arrows.

- The **Ctrl key** is used in combination with other keys. You'll probably see it represented like this: Ctrl-C. That means "press Ctrl and C at the same time." Pressing Ctrl-C is like pressing Esc; it bails you out of whatever's going on.

- The **Shift key** shifts you from lowercase to uppercase. DOS doesn't care which you use, so you can use either, or a combination of both.

- The **Print Screen key** (it may be marked Prt Sc) will send a copy of what's on your screen (called a screen dump) to your printer. Be sure to turn your printer on first.

- The **Alt key**, just under the Shift key, works like the Ctrl key: you press it in combination with other keys. When you see Alt-R, for example, press Alt and R and the same time.

- The **Pause** or **Break key** (you may have both of these, or just one) will stop whatever your computer's doing. If you don't have a Pause key, you can press Ctrl and Num Lock at the same time.

TIP— *DOS doesn't care whether you use uppercase or lowercase.*

TIP— *To restart your computer without actually turning the power off, press Ctrl, Alt, and Del, all at the same time. This is usually represented as Ctrl-Alt-Del.*

# The Mouse

You may or may not have a **mouse**. If I were you, I'd get one. Having a mouse makes DOS and most of your programs a lot more fun to use. If you're not sure whether you have a mouse, look for a rectangular object about the size of a cigarette pack attached by a cord to your computer. Technically, it's a pointing device that controls the position of the pointer on the screen. As you move the mouse on the desktop, the pointer moves on the screen. In DOS, the mouse only works when you're running the Shell or Editor, so we'll wait for the guided tour of the DOS Shell to practice your mouse skills.

> **TIP**— If you want to use a mouse, you'll need to have installed it according to the directions that came with it.

There are a couple of other things you may need to know about. One is about your disk drives and where they are. Why are they important? Think about it. All the programs you buy come on floppy disks, and they have to get onto your hard disk in some way. That's through your floppy disk drive.

# Disk Drives

Your computer has at least one floppy disk drive. The main one's called drive A. If you have two floppy disk drives, drive A's the one on the left. If one floppy disk drive is above the other, drive A is usually the one on the top.

> **TIP**— Store your floppy disks in a safe place that's relatively cool and dry. Keep them away from magnets! Magnets destroy whatever's on a disk.

The second floppy disk drive, if you've got one, is called drive B. Drive C is your hard disk. If you have more than one hard

## INSERTING DISKS

(fyi) When you put a disk in your floppy disk drive, slide it in with the label facing up and the little oval going into the drive first (if it's a 5.25-inch disk) or the metal shutter going into the drive first (if it's a 3.5-inch disk). Match the sizes to the slots: don't try to put one of the little 3.5-inch disks into a big 5.25-inch slot.

Then make sure you close the drive door, if you're using a 5.25-inch disk. Pull the door latch down. (On a 3.5-inch drive, the door will close when you push the disk in far enough.)

disk, or if you've divided a great big hard disk into smaller sections called partitions, the next drive's drive D, and so on.

Disk drives come in two sizes, one for 5.25-inch floppy disks and one for 3.5-inch floppy disks (which aren't very floppy; they're the little hard plastic ones). The little ones hold more data. And because they're harder, they're less likely to get damaged. They're also more expensive than the bigger ones. But you have to have a 3.5-inch disk drive to use them, and some computers (like the IBM XT) don't have that kind of drive as standard equipment. It's nicest when you have both types of drives—then you can use both kinds of disks.

# Memory and Storage

You hear "memory" discussed a lot, both in terms of disks and in terms of your computer. Here's the secret: there are two kinds of memory: **disk storage** and **random-access memory (RAM).** The kind of memory that's used for storage—on floppy and hard disks—isn't the same thing as the random-access memory (RAM) that's on chips in your computer. What's stored on disks stays there, even after you turn off your computer (that is, if you don't dump a cup of coffee on the disk or crumple it up or do something else nasty to it). What's in RAM is the information your computer is actually working with. When you turn off the computer (or when the lights go out), that information's gone if it hasn't been saved (stored) on disk yet. That's why it's important to save your work frequently when you work with programs.

To understand a little about memory and storage, you need to know how these things are measured. Both of them are rated in terms of bytes (a **byte** is one character). A thousand bytes (roughly) is a **kilobyte,** which is abbreviated K. A million bytes is a **megabyte,** which is abbreviated Mb.

Computers nowadays have at least 640K of random-access memory (RAM), and most have at least 1 Mb of RAM, but you don't need that much to run DOS itself. You can have much more random-access memory than this, and DOS will be happy to manage it for your programs. For example, to run DOS and Windows, you'll need 2 Mb of RAM to be comfortable (and even more is better).

Floppy disks typically store between 360K to 1.44 Mb of data. Your basic plain vanilla 5.25-inch floppy disk holds 360K, for example. And your hard disk probably holds 10 or 20 Mb or so, but it might be even larger: there are even 150-Mb hard disks out there.

Now, here's the practical difference between them. The more RAM you have, the more programs you can run at once. The bigger your hard disk, the more programs and data you can store. Got it? They're two different things.

You'll find out more details about disks and storage capacities in the Disks chapter. But for now, let's get to the guided tour right away.

If you see the C:\> prompt on your screen, type *dosshell* to start the Shell. If you're already at the Shell, you're ready to begin.

**TIP**— *DOS 6 comes with a disk compression program called Double-Space that makes extra space on your disks by compressing what's already there. See the appendix for how to install this feature.*

**2**

Sattinger's Law: It works better if you plug it in.
—ARTHUR BLOCH, *Murphy's Law*, 1977

# A Guided Tour

In this chapter we'll take a guided tour of the Shell so that you can quickly get familiar with it and practice the basic ways you interact with it. Start your computer so that you can follow along.

When you've got the Shell on your screen, you should see something that looks like this:

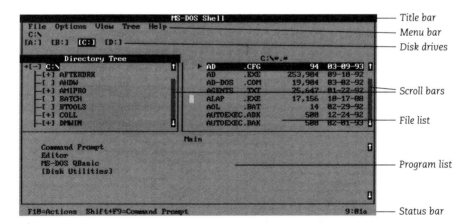

Yours will look a little different, because you'll have different files on your computer, of course. This screen is what usually appears if you haven't made any changes to the way DOS displays the Shell.

# Menu Bar

At the top of the screen is the Shell **menu bar**, showing File, Options, View, Tree, and Help. If you select any of these menus, you'll see more choices.

# Disk Drive Icons

Just underneath the menus are representations of your disk drives. Drive C, your hard disk, is highlighted, or displayed in reverse video. If you're looking at a graphics display, it will look

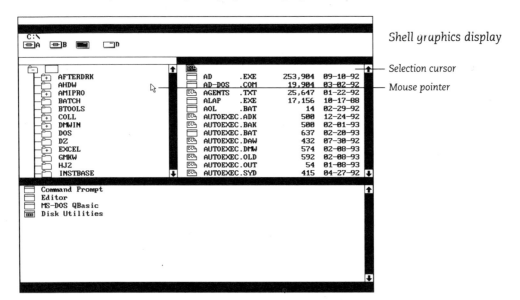

*Shell graphics display*

*Selection cursor*

*Mouse pointer*

prettier than a text screen. You'll see **icons,** or small pictorial representations, of your drives. (You'll see how to switch to a graphics display before you leave this chapter.)

# Directory Tree

The next area down, called the **directory tree,** lets you see at a glance how the files on your disks are organized. Everything that's on your computer is stored as a file—spreadsheets, graphic images, programs, documents: they're all files. Here DOS is listing the files that are on drive C. Each little box—or folder icon, if you're looking at a graphics display, represents a **directory,** or a collection of files. If it has a + on it, there are more directories, called **subdirectories,** underneath it.

# File List

To the right of the directory tree area is a list of all the files that are in the highlighted directory. Since only drive C is highlighted, the files listed here are the ones that are in the top-level directory of drive C. If you were to highlight another directory, you'd see a list of the files in it appear in this area, which is called (appropriately) the **file list**.

# Program List

At the bottom of the screen is the **program list**. This is a list of groups of programs. When you first use the Shell, it shows only the Main group, which contains the DOS Command Prompt, the Editor (a text editor), QBasic (a programming language), and the Disk Utilities program group, which contains several programs that let you format and copy disks, and undelete files you deleted by mistake.

## Program Groups

You can add programs to the Main group and the Disk Utilities group, or even create a group of your own. Being able to create groups of programs is one of the features of the Shell that makes it very much like Windows. If you use a program often, you can put it in a group along with documents that you use with it. Then you can start the program just by choosing the document you want to work with. No more "What was the name of that document?" and "Where did I save it?" or "What command do I use to start this program?" You'll see how later in the book, in the Programs chapter.

TIP— *Instead of looking at files and programs, you can look at just files or just programs. There are quite a few different choices on the View menu. You'll see different views in the Files, Directories, and Programs chapters.*

## Running Several Programs at Once

The Shell also lets you run several programs at once and switch between them. When a special feature called the **Task Swapper** is turned on (it's in the Options menu), the Shell screen changes to show you an active task list. You can then start programs running, and their names will appear in the

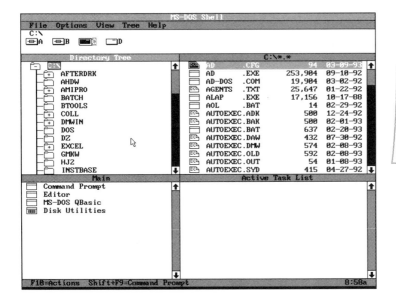

TIP— *When the Task Swapper's on, you'll see a list of all the programs you've got running in the Active Task List.*

task list. You can switch among them by pressing Alt-Tab. For example, you might want to have your spreadsheet program, a graphics program, and your word processor all loaded at the same time so that you can go back and forth and check data and graphics for a document you're writing. How many programs you can run at once depends on how much memory you've got. But because of the way DOS uses memory, folks, you can even do this on an XT!

# The Graphic Interface

The Shell is called a **graphic interface** because it lets you interact with your computer by **selecting** items that are represented on the screen instead of remembering cryptic commands.

# Selecting

To select menu items or icons, you can either use the keyboard or a mouse. It's more fun to use a mouse, so we'll look at that first. But you can use the Shell without a mouse. If you don't have one, skip the stuff about the mouse.

> **TIP—** You have to select something before you can work with it.

# Using a Mouse

A **mouse** is a pointing device that controls the position of the pointer on the screen. If you've installed your mouse properly, according to the instructions that came with it, you should see a small arrowhead or a shaded box on the Shell's screen. As you move the mouse on the desktop, the pointer moves on the screen. Try it and see.

> **TIP—** The mouse doesn't work in DOS outside the Shell. It won't work on the command line.

You can pick the mouse up! If you've pushed it all the way to the far corner of your desk and you're just about to knock over your coffee cup, just pick it up and put it down closer to you.

The pointer on the screen won't move. In fact, a lot of people get in the habit of just sort of keeping the mouse in place and scooting it a little way over and over again to move the screen pointer. If you haven't used a mouse before, try moving it and watching the pointer on the screen.

You use the mouse in three basic ways: by clicking, double-clicking, and dragging.

## Clicking

To select an item on the screen, you can move the mouse pointer to it and **click** once with the left mouse button. Once an item's selected, it's highlighted (and there's a tiny arrow next to it, on a text screen). For example, you might click on a folder icon so that you could see the files that are in that directory.

You can also just click in any of the different areas on the Shell screen to move into that area. This is a lot faster than using the keyboard to move between the different areas of the Shell's screen.

## Double-Clicking

You can **double-click** on some items to select them and start them at the same time. For example, you can double-click on the name of a program to start it running. To double-click, quickly click twice with the left mouse button.

You can also double-click on a program group icon to open it, or to close it once it's open.

## Shift-Clicking

You can Shift-click to select files that are next to each other. Just click on the first one, and then press and hold down the Shift key and click on the last one.

> **TIP**— The Files chapter will have more tips about selecting files.

You can hold down the Ctrl key while you click to select items that aren't next to each other.

## Dragging

Another way to use the mouse is by **dragging.** You can move files into different directories by dragging them. To drag, put the mouse pointer on what you want to move, press and hold the left button down, and then move the mouse. The item will move with it, if it can be moved. If you don't want to move the item but make a copy of it instead and leave the original where it is, press the Ctrl key while you drag.

TIP— *Press Ctrl and drag to copy.*

# The Keyboard

You can also use the Shell just with the keyboard, if you don't have a mouse, or you can switch back and forth and use a mouse for some things and the keyboard for others. That's what I do, because sometimes it's easier just to keep your hand on the keyboard instead of reaching for the mouse.

## Moving to Different Areas

The area you want to work in has to be active before you can work in it. To move from area to area on the screen with the keyboard, press Tab. The highlight will move, showing that the area's active. If you have a color monitor, the title bar will change color, too. Try it. Then press Shift-Tab to move the active area counterclockwise.

TIP— *Press Tab to move from area to area with the keyboard, or click with the mouse.*

## Selecting

Once you're within the area where you want to select something, you can use the arrow keys to move the highlight up or down. If you've selected a program, you can press Enter to start it; if it's a program group you've selected, you can open or close it by pressing Enter.

TIP— *If you're using a text screen instead of a graphics screen, there'll be a little arrow in the active area. Pressing Tab moves the tiny arrow clockwise from one area to the next.*

Try this now. Press Tab until you move into the Main Group area. If Disk Utilities isn't highlighted there, press the down arrow key until the highlight's on Disk Utilities. Then press Enter. You should then see a list of Disk Utilities, and you could choose one of them by highlighting it and pressing Enter. Highlight Main and press Enter to go back to where you were.

# Menus

The menus at the top of the screen let you perform actions on what you've selected. You can select a file and then choose Copy from the File menu, for example, to copy the file.

So what are these menus for? The commands on them let you carry out most of your everyday tasks, like copying files and disks. As you go further in the book, you'll find instructions for how to do these jobs and what to choose from the menus. In general, here's what the various menus do:

> TIP— Why is the shell called the Shell? Basically, because it surrounds the inner workings of your computer (the machine language part) and provides a way for you to give commands without having to use DOS commands at the command line.

- The **File menu** lets you run programs; give DOS commands; search for a file you're looking for; delete, copy, move, and rename files; and create directories for storing files in.

- The **Options menu** lets you change things about the way the Shell works, like whether you want to be prompted each time you delete a file or what information you want to see about your files on the screen. It also lets you change the screen colors, if you have a color monitor, and choose whether you want text or graphics display.

- The **View menu** controls whether you're looking at files on one disk or two, and whether you're looking at lists of programs, files, or both. It also lets you tell DOS to update the screen, if you've created new files in a program.

- The **Tree menu** lets you view your computer's filing system of directories and subdirectories. You can "expand" a directory to see what subdirectories are underneath it.

● The **Help menu** lets you get help on what you're doing. You'll see more about it later in this chapter.

To select from menus, you can use either the mouse, the keyboard, or a combination of both. To select from a menu with the mouse, just click on the menu name to open it. You can then click on the item you want to select it. Try it on the File menu. Click on File; then click on Run. (You can drag to it, too. Or you can just type the letter that's underlined or highlighted, like *d* for Delete on the File menu.) If you wanted to run a program, you'd type the command used to start it in the box that DOS shows you. Since you don't want to run a program now, click on Cancel or press Esc to get back to the regular display.

*TIP— Press Esc to cancel a menu.*

If you're using the keyboard to select from menus, press Alt (or F10) first. That selects the menu bar, even if you're in a different area of the screen. You can then use the right and left arrow keys to move to the menu you want to open and press Enter when it's highlighted.

Try this: Press Alt, press the right arrow key twice, and then press Enter to see what's on the View menu. Then press the left arrow key once to see what's on the Options menu. Press Esc to get back to the regular display.

*TIP— Here's a neat shortcut for selecting from menus: press Alt and type the first letter of the menu's name, like Alt-F for File. Then type the underlined or highlighted letter of the command you want to use. For example, Alt-F R opens the File menu and chooses Run.*

```
Open
Run...
Print
Associate...
Search...
View File Contents   F9

Move...               F7
Copy...               F8
Delete...             Del
Rename...
Change Attributes...


Select All
Deselect All

Exit                 Alt+F4
```

Once the menu is displayed, you can use the down arrow key to move to the item you want and press Enter, or you can type the special letter in the command. The second way's faster.

What you see on the menus depends on what you're doing. If you've selected a file, for example, you'll see a lot more choices on the File menu than you would if no file were selected. Try this now. Select any file in the file list (on the right side of the display); then select the File menu. Aha! More choices.

## Keyboard Shortcuts

Now you can see another little trick. Look at the File menu. In the second column, you'll see keys like F9 or Del listed. Those are **keyboard shortcuts** for the menu choice. For example, if you wanted to see what's in a highlighted file, you could just press F9. Back out of the File menu without choosing anything (press Esc or click somewhere else on the screen, out of the menu) and then press F9. (You may see garbage if the file you've selected isn't a text file.) Now, that's a handy thing to know about: you can take a peek at what's in a file without starting the program that created it. Press Esc to get back to the Shell screen.

Whenever you see a key listed to a menu choice, you can press it instead of using the menu system. You can also get online Help on them by choosing Keyboard from the Help menu. (You'll see more about the Help system later.)

If you see a diamond next to a menu item, that means it's active.

> **TIP**— *Sometimes items on a menu will be dimmed. That means you can't select that item at this time. You may have to select something else first—a file, for example.*

# Dialog Boxes

If you see … next to a menu item, it means that a **dialog box** will come up when you choose that item. If you choose Run... from the File menu, you'll see a dialog box where you can type the name of the program to run.

```
┌──────────────────── Run ────────────────────┐
│                                              │
│  Command Line . .  ┌──────────────────────┐  │
│                    └──────────────────────┘  │
│                                              │
│         (    OK    )      (   Cancel   )      │
│                                              │
└──────────────────────────────────────────────┘
```

Dialog boxes let you supply extra information that DOS needs. They can also give you warnings about what you're doing.

You can just press Esc or click on Cancel to get out of a dialog box without doing anything.

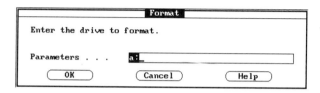

There are a lot of different kinds of dialog boxes. In some of them, you have to type **text,** like the Run dialog box. Some of them provide text that's already there, and if it's not what you want, you can type new text to replace it (just start typing; the new text will replace what's already there). For example, this dialog box assumes that you want to format a disk that's in drive A. You can just type B: to use drive B.

In others you can choose items from a **list.**

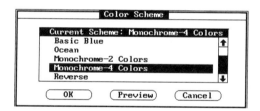

To select an item, highlight it with the arrow keys and then press Enter. If you've got a mouse, you can often just double-click on the item to select it and complete the command. This doesn't work in all dialog boxes, though.

Other kinds of dialog boxes let you choose command buttons. You can press Enter to choose OK or press Esc to select Cancel, or click with the mouse on either one. If you move from button to button with the keyboard, there'll be a tiny underline

on the button that's selected. Sometimes you have to look
closely to see it. You can press Enter to select it, too.

 To move from button to button, press Tab or an arrow key (or
just click with the mouse on the button you want).

Another kind of dialog box lets you choose only one option.
The option button that's selected has a tiny black dot:

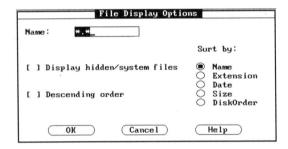

And yet another kind, called a **check box,** lets you choose several options at once (press the space bar to select these kinds
of items with the keyboard):

# Scroll Bars

Sometimes DOS can't display everything on the screen all at once. If that's the case, you'll see a **scroll bar** on the right of the area, like the one on the right of the directory tree area here.

TIP— *To scroll continuously with the mouse, click on one of the scroll arrows and hold the mouse button down until you see what you're looking for.*

Here's another place where the mouse is sometimes handier than the keyboard. To scroll the contents of the screen, you can click on the scroll arrows to move up or down one item at a time, or you can just drag the scroll box to about where you want to go. To go to the beginning of a long list, drag the scroll bar to the top. To go to the end, drag it to the bottom. Drag it to the middle to go to the middle. You get the idea.

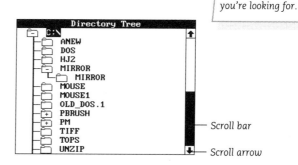

Scroll bar

Scroll arrow

If you're using the keyboard, you can press and hold down the up and down arrow keys to scroll, or you can use these keyboard shortcuts to move through lists:

**PgUp, PgDn**     To scroll one window up or down

**Home**     To go to the first item in a list

**End**     To go to the last item in a list

TIP— *Once an area is active, you can just type the first letter of an item's name to move directly to the first item in the list that begins with that letter. Very handy if you're looking for a file or directory beginning with W.*

# Customizing Your Display

Before you go any further with the Shell, there are a couple of things you can do to customize it as you'd like it.

If you have a graphics monitor, you can choose how DOS displays the Shell on your screen—whether you see icons, or whether you see just text. You'll probably want graphics. In addition, if yours is a color monitor, you can change the color scheme it uses.

## Graphics and Text Mode

Choose Display from the Options menu to see a Screen Display Mode dialog box. What you see will depend on your system, and you may need to scroll to see more choices. Choose Preview to see how each one looks. When you see a display you like, choose OK.

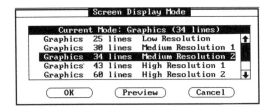

## Color Scheme

DOS comes with several predefined color schemes, and if you have a color monitor, you can pick different ones by choosing

**TIP**— *Even if you don't have a color monitor, you can choose two or four shades in monochrome, or choose reverse video.*

Colors from the Options menu. Scroll to see them all.

These are for a VGA monitor. Try Hot Pink for something truly garish. Emerald City's pretty wild, too. Basic Blue and Ocean are a little more restrained.

# Help!

There's one other very basic skill you need before you explore DOS on your own, and that's getting online help.

**TIP**— *The first time you use Help, choose Using Help so that you can get acquainted with the kind of help that's available.*

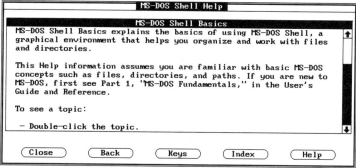

If you don't want help on a specific item, or if you don't know what you want help on, you can use the Help menu. Just press Alt-H or click on the Help menu.

**TIP**— *You don't have to be in the Shell to get help. At the command line, you can get help by entering /? after the command. For example, entering del /? gets you help on the DELETE command. Or you can type help, a space, and the name of the command you want help on and then press Enter.*

Choose Index to see a list of all the Help topics. If you choose Keyboard, you'll get a list of all the keyboard shortcuts you can use with the Shell. Choosing Commands gets you information on all the commands, and Procedures gives you instructions for how to do tasks in the Shell. Shell Basics gives you an introduction to using the Shell, and you might want to go through that now, just to review what you've learned in this chapter before you go on to the next.

**May all your wishes come true.**
—Ancient Irish Curse

# Entering Commands

DOS has a lot more commands than those that are represented in the Shell's menus. (They're all in the back of the book, in case you're interested.) The Shell just has commands for the things you do most often, like copying and moving files, formatting disks, and so on. But in the Shell you still sometimes have to fill out dialog boxes with whatever's needed to complete the command, like the new name you want a file to have, so you can't get completely avoid learning the rules you have to follow about entering commands.

You can give commands to DOS either from within the Shell (in dialog boxes) or at the command line (at the DOS prompt).

## Using the Command Line

To get to the command line from the Shell, press Shift-F9 or choose Command Prompt from the Main Group. You can just double-click on it with your mouse.

> **Tip**— To get back to the Shell after you've left it this way, type exit.

To enter a DOS command on the command line, you start with the **name** of the command, followed by what you want it to work on (the **parameters**). You can then add cryptic

**options** (sometimes called "switches") that let you specify how the command is to work. For example, in the command DIR A: /P, DIR is the command you're using to tell DOS to list a directory (DIR) of the files on drive A (A:) and to pause (/P) after each screen of files.

DIR A: /P

**Command**    **Parameters**    **Option**

TIP— *Neat trick: on the command line, to repeat a command that you just used, press F3.*

You'll find examples of how to enter each DOS command in the DOS Commands section in the back of this book. In particular, you'll see examples of how to use the options that let you specify just exactly how you want a task performed.

Keep a few things in mind when you enter commands on the command line:

- You enter commands at the DOS prompt (A:\>, C:\>, etc.). DOS types the A:\> or C:\>; you don't.

TIP— *To cancel a command you've typed before you press Enter, just press Esc.*

- You can use either caps or lowercase; DOS doesn't care which you use. I'm showing DOS commands in uppercase to distinguish them from the Shell menu commands.

- If you make a mistake while typing a command, backspace over it and correct it (the Backspace key is the one with the backward arrow on it, just above the Enter key).

- You have to press Enter after you've typed the command, so that DOS can read what you typed.

If you press Enter and you've entered the command wrong, you'll get a "bad command" message. Just re-enter it. DOS is very picky about how it wants things, and you have to be exact.

TIP— *Once a command is running, you can stop it by pressing Ctrl-C.*

You may get other messages, like "invalid directory" or "file not found." These usually mean that you didn't correctly specify the information the command needed.

# Entering Commands in the Shell

You can't get away from entering commands, even in the Shell! Although you choose the command you want from a menu, often the Shell just makes it easier by giving you a dialog box that's partially been filled out with what DOS thinks you want to do. For example, if you choose Copy from the File menu, DOS assumes that you want to copy it onto your hard disk, drive C, and gives you this dialog box:

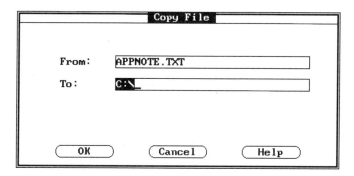

**TIP—** *You can copy by pressing Ctrl and dragging files with the mouse to avoid this dialog box.*

The name of the file you've highlighted has been filled in for you, and drive C and the directory you're in are filled in as the To: location. You can just type over what's being displayed, if it's not what you want. So you still have to know a few things about how to name files and such. (See the Files chapter for more on this.)

**TIP—** *You can use either uppercase or lowercase to enter text in the Shell's dialog boxes. It doesn't matter which.*

# Running DOS Commands with the Shell

You can choose Run from the File menu and give a DOS command there. You can run any program that way, too. (A DOS command is actually just a little program.) For example, if you wanted to delete a file named DOS.DOC, you could choose Run and enter the command DEL DOS.DOC in the Run dialog box and click O.K. Or if you wanted to run WordPerfect, you could just type *wp* there.

```
┌─────────────────────────────────────────────────────────┐
│                          Run                            │
│                                                          │
│  Command Line . .    ┌──────────────────────────────┐   │
│                      │ del dos.doc_                 │   │
│                      └──────────────────────────────┘   │
│                                                          │
│          ╭─────OK─────╮        ╭───Cancel───╮           │
└─────────────────────────────────────────────────────────┘
```

DOS will delete the file and ask you to press any key to return to the Shell. You can do this with the other DOS commands, too.

You can also choose Command Prompt from the Main group. This is the same as pressing Shift-F9, which takes you out to the command line until you type *exit* and press Enter to return to the Shell. This is the best way to run several DOS commands using the command line.

TIP—*This is a fast way to give a single DOS command without actually going out to the command line.*

## REMOVING THE SHELL FROM MEMORY

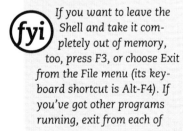

If you want to leave the Shell and take it completely out of memory, too, press F3, or choose Exit from the File menu (its keyboard shortcut is Alt-F4). If you've got other programs running, exit from each of them first, or you'll get a dialog box complaining at you. To exit from a program that you're running, use the method that you normally would in that program.

But if you're planning to come back to the Shell, exit by pressing Shift-F9. If you exit by pressing F3 or Alt-F4 or choosing Exit from the File menu, DOS will have to reread your hard disk if you start the Shell again.

To get back to the Shell if you've exited temporarily (with Shift-F9), type exit at the command prompt.

To get the Shell back after you've removed it from memory (with F3, Alt-F4, or the Exit command), type dosshell at the command prompt.

# Here's How To...

| | |
|---|---|
| **Get to the command line from the Shell** | Choose Command Prompt from the Main group, or press Shift-F9. To get back, type *exit*. |
| **Cancel a command before you've entered it** | Press Esc |
| **Repeat a command at the command line** | Press F3 |
| **Correct a command before you've entered it** | Press Backspace and type the correction |
| **Enter a command after you've typed it** | Press Enter |
| **Get online help at the command line** | Type the command's name followed by /? or *help* followed by the command |
| **Pause a command** | Press Ctrl-S or Pause |
| **Stop a command** | Press Ctrl-C or Ctrl-Break |
| **Remove the Shell from memory** | Choose Exit from the File menu, or press F3 or Alt-F4 |
| **Get the Shell back after it's been taken out of memory** | Type *dosshell* at the command prompt |

**Rain does not fall on one roof alone.**

—CAMEROON PROVERB

# Files

Everything you store on your computer is stored as a **file.** Your word processing documents are stored as files, and so are your spreadsheets. In fact, your programs themselves are special types of files called executable files, because they run (or "execute").

## Creating a File

How do you create a file? Normally, you use a program like WordPerfect or Quattro Pro or PC Paintbrush, although you can create text files (including a special kind of file called a batch file) by using the text editor supplied with DOS. (It's appropriately called the Editor, and there's more about using it in the AUTOEXEC.BAT chapter.) When you save the file (store it on disk), you're asked to name it, and that creates the file.

**TIP—** *There's one other way to create a file: by copying it from the keyboard as you type. See COPY in the DOS Commands section if you want to know how to do this.*

# Naming Files

DOS makes you follow rigid rules about naming files. You can only use eight characters, so you have to be creative and compress enough information into the name so that you can identify the file again. Here are the characters you can use: all the alphabet (DOS thinks uppercase and lowercase are the same thing), all the numbers, and the characters $ ~ # @ ! ' ( ) { } - _ ^.

Don't ever use these, though:

|  |  |
|---|---|
| < > | angle brackets |
| \ | backslash |
| \| | bar |
| [ ] | brackets |
| : | colon |
| , | comma |
| = | equals |
| + | plus |
| " " | quotation marks |
| ; | semicolon |
| / | slash |

**TIP**— *If you use a name that's longer than eight characters, DOS will just chop it off without telling you. MARYLET-TER becomes MARYLETT, for example. This can cause a problem if you already have a MARYLETT file.*

So you can name a file BOBLETTR or BOB_LTR or BOB, but not BOB LETTER or "BOB's" or BOB*LET.

**TIP**— *Be careful not to name a file with the same name as another file in the same directory. You'll get an "access denied" message if you do.*

Set up a consistent naming system so that you can identify your files weeks and even months after you've saved them. For example, you might want to name a letter you wrote on the second of February as 2_2LET. Or you might want to use the name of the person you wrote the letter to, like SMITHLET. If you're consistent about following a system, you'll stand a better chance of being able to figure out which file is which later.

## Extensions

In addition to the eight characters you can use for file names, you'll often see a period and three more characters. This is called an **extension** because it's an addition to the file's basic name. Extensions are used to help identify what kind of file it is. For example, programs always have an extension of .EXE or .COM, like WP.EXE for WordPerfect. Most programs automatically add a special extension to the file name when you save the document or spreadsheet or graphic you're working on, so that it's identified as belonging to that program. WordStar uses .WSD, Lotus 1-2-3 uses .WKS, Excel uses .XLS, and so forth.

> **Tip—** *Extensions are especially important in DOS, because they let you associate files with the programs that created them. Once you've associated files with the programs they belong to, you can start the program running and open the file at the same time. You'll see how in the Programs chapter.*

In the Shell, program files have icons that are different from document files. Look closely. Program files have a line across the top, while document files look like tiny dog-eared documents. (You have to be looking at a medium- or low-resolution graphics screen to see this.)

# Changing File Names

OK, you've named a file. Then you decide that you want to change its name. Maybe somebody gave you the file and you want to rename it to suit your file-naming system. Or maybe you're setting up a new system of file names and want to change a lot of them at the same time. Here's how.

## Renaming a File

To rename a file, highlight it and choose Rename from the File menu. You'll see a dialog box asking you to type the new name. After you do that (be sure to follow the rules), choose OK, or just press Enter.

> **Tip—** *You can also use the DOS REN command (for RENAME) to rename a file.*

Once you rename a file, it moves to a new alphabetical position in the file list. To see it, just type the first letter of its new name to move to that part of the alphabet.

## Renaming a Bunch of Files

You can rename a bunch of files in the Shell at the same time by selecting them and then choosing Rename from the File menu. DOS will give you a dialog box asking for the new name of each one.

# Selecting Files

Selecting a single file is easy: just click on it with the mouse or highlight it with the arrow keys. What gets tricky is when you want to select more than one file.

## Selecting Adjacent Files

You can select files that are next to each other by Shift-clicking with the mouse. To Shift-click, click on the first file you want; then hold down the Shift key and click on the last file you want.

With the keyboard, move to the first file you want by using the arrow keys; then press Shift (hold it down) and move to the last file you want.

```
APPENDIX              10,715   04-08-91
BATCH                 18,805   01-03-91
CH1                   17,749   04-04-91
CH1-3     .PPP         8,777   01-21-91
CH10                  25,945   04-08-91
CH11                  92,420   04-09-91
CH2                   25,822   04-07-91
CH3                   11,088   04-04-91
```

There are other keyboard shortcuts for selecting without a mouse. (Check out Help.) But it's so much easier with a mouse!

TIP— *Press Home to select the first file in a list or End to select the last one. Type the first letter of a file's name to move to that area of the alphabet.*

TIP— *Pressing Ctrl-/ or choosing Select All from the File menu will select all the files in a list. Ctrl-\ or Deselect All will unselect all but the last file you selected.*

## Selecting Nonadjacent Files

You can even select files that aren't next to each other. To do this, Ctrl-click with the mouse on all the items you want. If you're using the keyboard, first turn on Add mode by pressing Shift-F8. You can then use the arrow keys to move to each item and press the space bar to select it. Press Shift-F8 when all the items are selected.

TIP— *To select files that are in different directories, choose Select Across Directories from the Options menu (press Alt-O and type A to use a keyboard shortcut for this).*

| | | | |
|---|---|---|---|
| CH1 | | 17,749 | 04-04-91 |
| CH1-3 | .PPP | 8,777 | 01-21-91 |
| CH10 | | 25,945 | 04-08-91 |
| CH11 | | 92,420 | 04-09-91 |
| CH2 | | 25,822 | 04-07-91 |
| CH3 | | 11,088 | 04-04-91 |
| CH3 | .TWG | 6,946 | 04-08-91 |

## Deselecting Files

Suppose you select a file by mistake? No problem. To deselect one file, press Ctrl and click on it, or, in Add mode, move to it with the arrow keys and use the space bar to deselect it. To deselect all but one file, click on that file. To cancel all selections but the last one, press Ctrl-\ or choose Deselect All.

# Deleting Files

Sooner or later, you'll want to delete a file or two. For one thing, you'll eventually run out of room on your disk.

In the Shell, just select the file or files you want to delete and press Del, or choose Delete from the File menu. You'll be prompted about whether you really want to delete the files.

On the command line, you don't get any notice that a file has actually been deleted, but if you try to get a directory listing of it with the DIR command, you'll get the message "file not found." In the Shell, you'll see the file disappear from the screen, if you look closely.

WARNING— *DOS will display only the file names that are in the current directory, so you won't be able to see all the files you've selected if you've selected across directories. It's easy to delete files by mistake this way.*

You can also copy files and move them as well as delete them. See Chapter 5, "Directories and Subdirectories," for more about copying and moving files, because you'll usually do that from one directory to another.

> **TIP—** At the command line, use DEL or ERASE to delete files. Use DELTREE to delete directories. See the DOS Commands chapter for details.

# Looking at Different File Views

You can use the View menu to specify whether you want to look at lists of files as well as programs (this is the preset choice, Program/File Lists) or whether you want to view just files, or just programs.

## Single File List

If you choose Single File List from the View menu, you'll see just the directory tree and a list of the files in the current directory. As you select each directory in the directory tree window, the file list will change to show the files that are in it.

The file's size (in bytes) and the date it was created or most recently changed is shown next to the file's name.

> **TIP—** On your computer, files are organized into a system of directories and subdirectories, like file folders. You'll see more about them in the Directories chapter.

## UNDELETING FILES

If you didn't really mean to delete a file, you can get it back (if you realize it soon enough). DOS doesn't actually delete a file from the disk; it just marks the space the file takes up as reusable. So if you haven't done a lot of work between the time you deleted the file and the time you realize that you didn't want to do that, you can probably get the file back.

To undelete a file you just deleted, choose Undelete from the Disk Utilities group. You'll get a warning that you might lose the file under some conditions, but if you need it back, what have you got to lose? It's already deleted. Go ahead and press Enter to see a list of files you can undelete (you'll be taken to the command line). Make a note of the file or files you want to recover, because there may be quite a few of them listed if you're using DOS 6's new Delete Sentry protection (see Chapter 8 if this doesn't ring a bell).

Now, with the name of the file you want to undelete in hand, press a key to return to the Shell. Choose Undelete again and enter the file's name in the Undelete box, replacing the /LIST that's already there. This time, you'll

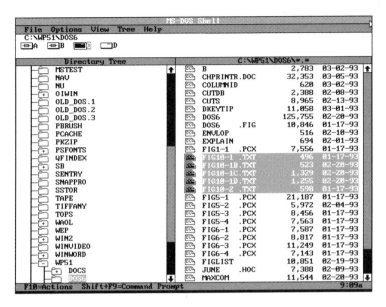

*Single File List*

**TIP—** *Using Single File List is like getting a directory listing with the DOS DIR command. You get the same information about the files in the current directory as you do with that command.*

Choosing All Files lets you see all the files on a disk, listed alphabetically, as well as their size, and when they were created or changed. It also shows information about the size of the disk (in bytes), how many files are on it, how much space is

be asked whether you want to undelete that file. Type **y** for Yes.

You can speed up this process a bit if you already know the name of the file you want to undelete. Just enter it in place of the /LIST in the Undelete dialog box.

Instead of using the Disk Utilities group, you can also go to the command line and give the UNDELETE command with the name of the file you

deleted by mistake. Remember to specify the drive the file you're undeleting is on if it's on a disk in a different drive.

If by any chance you're not using DOS 6's new deletion protection schemes, you may still be able to get your deleted file back. If DOS reports that it's using the "MS-DOS directory method," enter **undelete /dos** at the command line.

You'll see the file name with a ? as the first character

of its name. Type Y to undelete it. You'll then be asked for the first letter of its name; just type any character (such as @), and DOS will undelete it.

You can also use wildcards to undelete groups of files that have similar names. For example, if you deleted a group of files that all ended in .DOC, you could get them back with UNDELETE *.DOC.

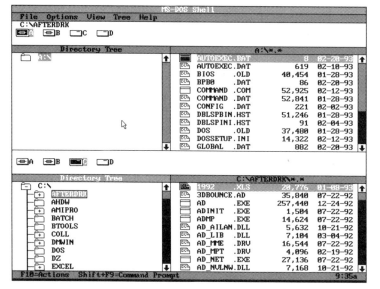

All Files

available, how many directories are there, and so forth. As you select each different file, the area on the left changes to show information about the directory the file is in.

Dual File List

If you choose Dual File List, you can see files and directories on two disks, or look at two directories on the same disk. This is handy for when you want to copy or move files from one directory to another.

## Getting More Information

To get detailed information about a file, select it and choose Show Information from the Options menu. You'll then see an information window about the file showing its name, size, and attributes (more on these soon).

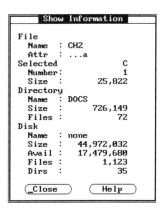

The Show Information window also tells you the directory's name and size, the size of the disk and number of files on it, the number of directories on the disk, and the space available.

**TIP**— *Choose Show Information to see how much space is left on a disk.*

## File Attributes

**Attributes** are special characteristics of a file that you don't normally have to worry about. They indicate to DOS exactly what type of file it is and a few other things about it. Here are the attributes a file can have:

**TIP**— *Look up ATTRIB in the DOS Commands section to see more details about file attributes.*

- Hidden—hides the file so that it doesn't appear in a directory listing.

- System—indicates that the file is a DOS system file.

- Archive—indicates whether a file has been used lately.

- Read only—indicates that the file can't be changed.

**TIP**— *Giving a file the hidden attribute hides it from directory listings so that casual browsers can't see it.*

Most of the time you probably won't need to change a file's attributes, but you can do this quite easily in the Shell (or by using the DOS ATTRIB command). Just select the files whose attributes you want to change (Shift-click for adjacent files, Ctrl-click for files that aren't next to each other) and then select Change Attributes from the File menu. You can then choose whether you want to change the files one at a time or all at once (if you're changing the same attribute on all the files). After that, you can choose which attribute to change and then press Enter. A small symbol next to the attribute indicates that it's on.

Giving a file the read-only attribute is a neat trick for keeping files from being changed by other people (and yourself). If you share a computer with others, you'll appreciate this trick.

You might want to make a file hidden or read-only to protect it from getting altered, but the other two attributes are best left to DOS. The archive attribute's important so that DOS can keep track of which files have been backed up, and the system file attribute indicates that a file is part of DOS.

*TIP— Making a file read-only doesn't stop people from reading what's in it. It just stops them from changing it or erasing it. It stops you, too, by the way.*

## Sorting the File List

To choose how you want your files displayed, select File Display Options from the Options menu. You can get them sorted in reverse alphabetical order, sort them by size (largest to smallest), sort them by date (most recent first), and so forth.

*TIP— Getting a list that's sorted by date lets you quickly find the files you worked on most recently.*

```
┌──────────┤ File Display Options ├──────────┐
│                                             │
│  Name :   ▮*.*▮_____                  │
│                                             │
│                          Sort by:           │
│                                             │
│  [ ] Display hidden/system files  ◉ Name    │
│                                   ○ Extension│
│                                   ○ Date     │
│  [ ] Descending order             ○ Size     │
│                                   ○ DiskOrder │
│                                             │
│     (    OK    )   (  Cancel  )   (  Help  )  │
│                                             │
└─────────────────────────────────────────────┘
```

# Finding Files

Instead of looking through all the different directories and file views to find the file you're looking for, you can use the Shell's Search command to find a file, as long as you know part of its name.

When you choose Search from the File menu, you'll see a dialog box that lets you type the name of the file you're looking for. If you know its name, fine; if you can guess at part of its name, use **wildcards.**

In poker, wildcards match anything. In DOS, they stand for the letters in the name that all the files have in common. In DOS, the ? stands for any one character, and the ★ stands for any number of characters. So A★ means "all files beginning with A (with no extension)" and A★.★ means "all files beginning with A and with any extension."

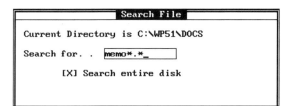

```
╔══════════════╡ Search File ╞══════════════╗
║                                            ║
║  Current Directory is C:\WP51\DOCS         ║
║                                            ║
║  Search for. .   memo*.*_                  ║
║                                            ║
║           [X] Search entire disk           ║
║                                            ║
╚════════════════════════════════════════════╝
```

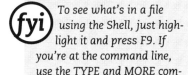

## SEEING WHAT'S IN A FILE

To see what's in a file using the Shell, just highlight it and press F9. If you're at the command line, use the TYPE and MORE com-

mands to see what's in a file (see the DOS Commands section for how).

A lot of the time what you see will be garbage, though. This is because programs add special formatting characters to their files. If the file is a special kind of file called a

text-only file (sometimes called an **ASCII file**), you'll be able to read it just fine. If it's a file you've created with a word processing program, you'll be able to read parts of it, but there'll be lots of weird formatting characters.

LETTER?.DOC means all files beginning with LETTER and ending in a single character, like LETTER1.DOC, LETTERA.DOC, or LETTER_.DOC.

For example, you may be looking for a file that you know starts with MEMO. Enter MEMO*.* to search for all files beginning with MEMO and ending in anything. Or enter *.EXE to search for all the program (executable) files.

When the search is over, DOS will display all the files that matched the name or the pattern you entered. You can select each one and press F9 to see what's inside it (but this often won't tell you much). Press Esc to get back to the Shell.

**TIP**— *If you're looking for specific lines in the text of a file, use the FIND command. See the DOS Commands section for details.*

```
 File   Options   View   Tree   Help
                     Search Results for: MEMO*.*
[icon]   C:\PM\TEMPLATE\MEMO.PT3
[icon]   C:\PM\MEMORY.EXE
[icon]   C:\WP51\MASTER\CH7\MEMO.WPM
[icon]   C:\WP51\DOCS\MEMO.PF
```

**WARNING**— *Although *.* appears in the Search dialog box, don't search for it (*.* means "everything"). That would be meaningless, if you think about it. But this is what DOS will do if you don't enter a file name or a different wildcard pattern.*

# What Else Can You Do with Files?

You can copy and move them from one directory to another. See the Directories chapter.

**TIP**— *Searching the whole disk can take a while, depending on how many files you've got. If you've got a general idea of which directories the file might be in, just search those by unchecking Search Entire Disk, highlighting each directory in turn, and searching it.*

# *Here's How To...*

| | |
|---|---|
| **Create a file** | Save it in a program |
| **Name files** | Use eight characters plus a three-character extension |
| **Change file names** | Select the file and choose Rename from the File menu (or use the DOS REN command) |
| **Select all files** | Press Ctrl-/ or choose Select All from the File menu |
| **Select adjacent files** | Shift-click, or press Shift and use the arrow keys |
| **Select nonadjacent files** | Ctrl-click, or press Shift-F8, (Add mode), use the arrow keys to move to each file, press the space bar to select it, and press Shift-F8 again when you're done |
| **Move files** | Drag them, or press F7, or choose Move from the File menu |
| **Copy files** | Ctrl-drag them, or press F8, or choose Copy from the File menu (or use the DOS COPY or XCOPY commands) |
| **Deselect all files** | Press Ctrl-\ or choose Deselect All from the File menu |

| | |
|---|---|
| **Deselect all but one file** | Click on it, or, in Add mode, move to it with the arrow keys and press the space bar |
| **Delete files** | Select the files and choose Delete from the File menu, or press Del (or use the DOS DEL or ERASE commands) |
| **See just a list of files in the current directory** | Choose Single File List from the View menu (or use the DOS DIR command) |
| **Get information about a file** | Choose Show Information from the Options menu |
| **Choose how files are displayed** | Choose File Display Options from the Options menu |
| **Protect a file from being changed** | Select Change Attributes from the File menu and choose the Read Only attribute |
| **See files on two disks, or files in two directories on the same disk** | Choose Dual File List from the View menu |
| **See all files on a disk** | Choose All Files from the View menu |
| **Use wildcards** | The ? represents one character, and the * represents any number of characters or none at all |
| **See what's in a file** | Select the file and press F9 (or use the DOS TYPE command) |

| | |
|---|---|
| **See just a list of files in the current directory** | Choose Single File List from the View menu (or use the DOS DIR command) |
| **Search for a file by name** | Choose Search from the File menu and enter the name or the pattern of the name, using wildcards |
| **Select a file** | Click on it or use the arrow keys to highlight it |
| **Go to the first or last file in a list** | Press Home or End |
| **Go to an area of the alphabet in a list** | Type the letter |
| **Undelete a file** | Choose Undelete from the Main group and give the name of the file to undelete, or press Enter to see a list of files that can be undeleted (or use the DOS UNDELETE command) |

They drew all manner of things—everything
that begins with an M... such as mouse-traps,
and the moon, and memory, and muchness...

—LEWIS CARROLL, *Alice's Adventures in Wonderland*, 1865

# Directories and Subdirectories

On your computer, files are organized into a system of
**directories**. Think of a directory as a file folder in a filing cabinet. You can put all kinds of files in a directory—program
files, spreadsheets, documents, graphic images, whatever you
like. Directories can even hold other directories, called **subdirectories**, just like you stuff folders inside other folders in
a filing cabinet. For example, you might have a directory
named LOTUS and a subdirectory beneath it named SALES
where you kept sales spreadsheets. The entire structure of directories and subdirectories is called the **directory tree,** but
it's an upside-down tree with the root on top! Like a lot of
things about computers, it's upside down.

> **TIP**—*The directory you're
> in is called the current
> directory. In the Shell,
> it's the folder that's high-
> lighted, and you see its
> name over the disk drive
> icons at the top. The
> current drive is the one
> that's highlighted at the
> top of the screen.*

## The Root Directory

At the top of your directory system is what DOS calls the **root
directory.** All the other directories and their subdirectories
branch off from it.

When you start the Shell, you always start in the root
directory. In the directory tree, it's represented by a folder that

> **TIP**—*The \ is shorthand
> for the root directory,
> and that's why you
> can't use it in a file
> name.*

has C:\ next to it. The C indicates that you're on drive C, your hard drive.

On the command line, when you get that C:\> prompt, or some variation of it, you're at the root directory.

**TIP**— *On the command line, you change drives by typing the drive letter, typing a colon (:), and pressing Enter. So if the prompt says A:\>, to change to C:\>, you'd type C: and press Enter. You change directories with the CD command.*

Root directory ———

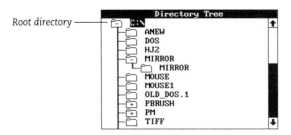

# Seeing What's in Directories

In the Shell, to see what's in a directory, you can either click on it or use the up and down arrow keys to move through the list of folders. As you move through the folders, the file list on the right changes to show the files that are in them.

## Expanding and Collapsing Directories

A tiny + on a folder means that there's at least one subdirectory beneath it. If you click once on the folder with the mouse or highlight it and type a +, the display will change so that you can see these hidden subdirectories, and the + will change to a –. This is called **expanding** a directory, and the opposite— closing everything up again—is called **collapsing** a directory. You can expand all your directories at once, so that you see your entire file structure at a glance (well, everything that will fit in one window), or you can expand just one "branch" of a directory and its related subdirectories.

**TIP**— *At the command line, DIR is the command you use to see what's in directories.*

To do this, you use the Tree menu. For example, if you wanted to expand one branch, you'd highlight the folder you want to look in and then choose Expand Branch or type an

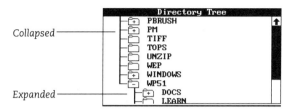

Collapsed

Expanded

asterisk (*). That will expand all the subdirectories under it.
To expand *just one level* of subdirectories, choose Expand One
Level, or type a +. To expand *all* the folders in the directory
tree window, choose Expand All, or press Ctrl-*.

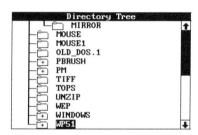

## Looking at What's on Other Drives

DOS automatically shows you what's on drive C, but you can
click on one of the tiny drive icons at the top of the Shell
screen to view what's on a floppy disk in one of your floppy
disk drives. To use a keyboard shortcut, press Ctrl and type the
drive letter. (Your floppy disk drives are always called A and
B.) If there's no disk in the drive when you do this, you'll get
a "drive not ready" message.

Here's a neat trick. Suppose you want to see what's on the
disks in drive A and look in directories on drive C at the same
time. Choose Dual File Lists from the View menu. DOS will
then split the screen in two and you can then click on the icon
of the disk drive that has the other disk you want to take a look
at. You can use this trick to display two directories that are on
the same disk, too. Or look at what's on drives A and B.

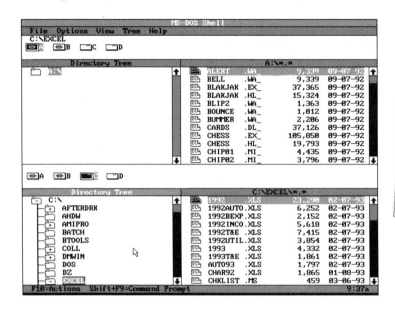

TIP— *To reread what's on a disk (if you've taken one disk out of the drive and put another in, for example), double-click on the drive icon at the top of the screen, or highlight it and press the space bar. Pressing F5 is the keyboard shortcut; it refreshes the screen.*

## Looking at All the Files on a Disk

Normally the DOS Shell shows you all the directories that are on your hard drive plus any program groups that you've set up (the Programs chapter will tell you how to do this). This is the Program/File Lists display.

You can get a big, full-screen display of everything that's on a disk by selecting the drive and choosing All Files from the View menu. This also gets you a window that has information

## WHOOPS! GENERAL FAILURE?

*Sometimes DOS may refuse to show you what's on a floppy disk. If you put a blank disk in drive A, you'll get a message saying "General Failure." Don't panic; that just means that the disk hasn't been formatted yet. If you get a message saying that the drive isn't ready, you probably forgot to close the drive door, or you may have put the disk in the drive upside down, or you may have put a high-density disk in a regular disk drive (see the Disks chapter for more about types of disks and drives and how to tell them apart). Take the disk out and look at it. If it's a 5.25-inch disk, you need to put it in with the label face up and the oval cutout going in first. If it's a 3.5-inch disk, the metal shutter has to go in first. And remember to close the 5.25-inch disk drive door.*

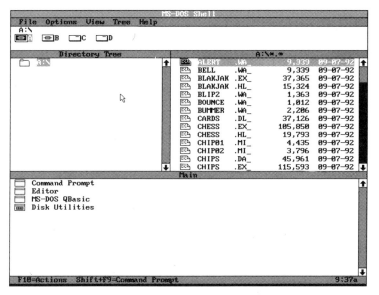

*Program/File Lists display*

about the disk, like how many files are on the disk and how much space is left on it.

Once you've got the All Files display, you'll see the files in the disk, in alphabetical order (names that start with numbers will

*All Files display*

**TIP**— It's often handy to know how much space is left on a disk if you're trying to figure out whether it can hold more files.

**TIP**— You can choose Show Information from the Options menu to get detailed information about a file that you've selected.

come first). You can then choose File Display Options from
the Options menu and get the files listed by date (most recent
first), by size, sorted in reverse order, or listed from largest to
smallest, or even sorted into the order that they are on the disk.

## Looking at Different Directory Views

So maybe you don't need to see everything that's on a disk,
just what's in a directory. The Shell shows files organized by
directories when you choose Program/File Lists, Single File
List, or Dual File List from the View menu.

TIP— *If you're looking
for a file often, rename
it to begin with a
number. That way it'll
always be at the top of
the file list. Don't do this
with your program files,
though; just your docu-
ments.*

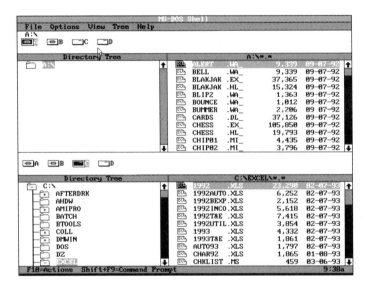

Dual File List display

TIP— *Choose Dual File
List if you're copying or
moving files from one
directory to another.
You can see into both
directories.*

If you just want to see the directory tree on the left and a list
of what files are in the selected directory, choose Single File
List. As you select different directories, the file list will change
to reflect what's in them.

## Looking at Groups of Files

Well, maybe you don't want to look at all of the files in a directory. Directories can get pretty big. You can just look at just

the files that have a certain extension or a certain pattern to their names.

The trick here is to again use the File Display Options dialog box. It lets you specify which files you want to look at. You can use the special wildcard characters to stand for the letters in the name that all the files have in common. Remember, the ? stands for any one character, and the * stands for any number of characters. So to see all the files that end in .WPG, you'd enter *.WPG. To see all the files beginning with A and ending with anything, you'd enter A*.*. Or to see all the files that have the pattern MEMO1, MEMO2, MEMO3, and so forth, you'd enter MEMO?.

> **TIP—** DOS assumes that you always want to see everything, and that's what the *.* at the top of the file list and after Name: in the File Display Options dialog box stands for. This *.* is a wicked little trick. It means "everything."

```
╔══════════════════════════════════════════╗
║          File Display Options             ║
║                                            ║
║  Name:      *.wpg_                          ║
║                                            ║
║                         Sort by:           ║
║  [ ] Display hidden/system files   ⦿ Name  ║
║                                    ○ Extension
║                                    ○ Date   ║
║  [ ] Descending order              ○ Size   ║
║                                    ○ DiskOrder
║                                            ║
║   ( OK )      ( Cancel )     ( Help )       ║
╚══════════════════════════════════════════╝
```

## THE PATH

The notation at the top of the file list is the **path** to the directory you're in—the current directory. The command line prompt also always shows the path to the directory you're in (see PROMPT in the DOS Commands section). The path is the way DOS (and you) can keep track of where things are, if you've got subdirectories within subdirectories. The path is just a list of all the directories that lead to the directory that holds the file you're looking for, just like the house that Jack built.

What's confusing about paths is the cryptic way you have to write them out. You use a backslash to separate each directory name, and you have to remember to put a colon (:) after the drive letter. So C:\WP51\DOCS indicates the DOCS subdirectory of the WP51 directory, which is under the root directory (the first \). And A:\CHAPTERS indicates a directory on the disk in drive A (yes, you can have directories on floppy disks, too). In the Shell, you don't have to worry too much about paths because you can usually just choose which folder you want to look in, or drag documents to other folders to copy and move them. You may have to type paths sometimes, though—if the directory you're copying a file into isn't visible on the screen, for example, or if you don't have a mouse.

# Creating a Directory

You can create directories of your own and add them to the structure that's already on your hard disk. When you choose Create Directory from the File menu (or press Alt-F and type *e*), you'll see a dialog box listing the directory that's currently highlighted. This is called the **parent directory,** because the new directory you create (the **child**) will be underneath it. If you don't want to create your new directory there, highlight the directory you want the new directory to go under, or highlight the root directory to put the new directory up at the top of your directory tree.

**TIP**— *At the command line, you create directories with the MD (Make Directory) command. The XCOPY command will create directories, too. See the DOS Commands section for details.*

**TIP**— *Quickest way to get back to the root directory in the directory tree window: just press Home.*

When you create a directory, DOS doesn't automatically make it current. Select it to make it current.

# Removing a Directory

In the Shell, it's easy. Just highlight the directory you want to delete and press Del. You'll get prompted to make sure that's really what you want to do.

If there's anything in the directory, you'll get an error message. Go back and delete any files or subdirectories that are in the directory; you'll be able to delete it then.

At the command line, to delete a single directory with no subdirectories, you can use the RD (Remove Directory) command. You'll need to delete any files that are in it first, and you'll need to change out of it (with the CD command) before you can delete it. Use the command **DEL \*.\*** to delete everything in a directory (remember, \*.\* means "everything").

DOS 6 added an even neater command, DELTREE, for deleting entire directories and subdirectories. You have to use it at the command line.

## DELTREE

The new DELTREE command lets you erase entire directories as well as all the files and subdirectories that are in them, all at the same time.

To delete a directory, just use this command: **DELTREE *directory name*.** For example, to delete the directory named C:\DOCS, just enter **deltree c:\docs**.

Use DELTREE carefully. You can delete more than you realize. Say that you want to delete your C:\DOCS directory and all its subdirectories—C:\DOCS\LETTERS, C:\DOCS\-MEMOS, C:\DOCS\REPORTS, C:\DOCS\REPORTS\AUGUST, and so forth. Just entering **deltree c:\docs** will delete these directories and subdirectories and all the files in them if you type **y** to confirm that you want to delete "docs" and all its subdirectories. To be careful, change to each directory you're deleting and use the DIR command it see if there are any files in any of those directories that you want to keep. If there are, copy them into a different directory before using DELTREE.

# Moving a Directory

DOS 6 greatly streamlines the process of moving a directory. Before, to move a directory from one location to another, you had to create a new directory, copy files into it from the old directory, and then delete the old directory. What a chore!

**TIP—** *You can't rename a directory with the DOS REN command. Use MOVE instead.*

When you move a directory, what you're basically doing is *renaming* it. Just give the old name first and then the new name:

**move c:\\*oldname* c:\\*newname***

So, to rename C:\DOCS as C:\REPORTS, use **move c:\docs c:\reports.**

In the Shell, renaming directories is even easier: Highlight the directory; then choose Rename and enter the new name. Follow the same rules as file names. Two subdirectories in the same directory can't have the same name.

> **TIP—** *The MOVE command only lets you move directories at the same level. You can't, for example, move c:\docs c:\reports\docs, because that would put the DOCS directory one level deeper down in the hierarchy. You can move files to different levels, just not directories.*

# Copying and Moving Files in Directories

You'll often want to reorganize your files into different directories. Before you can copy or move a file, though, you have to select it. The Files chapter has a lot of tips for selecting files, whether they're next to each other or all over the place.

> **TIP—** *Choose Dual File Lists to see into two directories at once.*

Once you've selected a file (or a group of files), you can use the File menu's Copy and Move commands to put them in other directories, or you can just drag them to their new locations with the mouse, if the destination folder's visible on the screen. Drag to move; Ctrl-Drag to copy.

## Moving Files

If you have a mouse, moving files is really easy in the Shell. Once the file and the directory it's going to be moved into are both visible on the screen, just select the file and drag it into its new directory. If you have Confirm on Mouse Operation checked in the Confirmation options dialog box, you'll be asked to verify that this is what you want to do.

> **TIP—** *Alt-drag to move; Ctrl-drag to copy.*

With the keyboard, select the file you want to move and then choose Move from the File menu, or press F7. You'll see the Move dialog box.

```
┌────────────────── Move File ──────────────────┐
│                                                │
│   From:    CALENDAR.WPG                        │
│   To:      C:\WP51_                            │
│                                                │
│                                                │
│      ( OK )        ( Cancel )        ( Help )  │
└────────────────────────────────────────────────┘
```

DOS will display the name of the directory that's highlighted. If that's not where you want to move the file, type the path to the directory where you want to move it to and then choose OK.

You can move several files at once if you've selected them first. Choose Select Across Directories from the Options menu to move files from several directories at once. If you're using a mouse, the icons will change to a tiny stack of documents as you drag the last selected file.

## Moving Files with the New MOVE Command

DOS 6 adds a new MOVE command-line command that lets you easily move files. When you move a file, it disappears from its current location and appears in the new location. Don't confuse MOVE with COPY. With COPY, the original file stays where it is and you get a duplicate of it in the new location.

For example, to move a file named REPORT.TXT that's in the current directory to another directory named C:\DOCS\MARCH, you'd just type this at the command line:

**move report.txt c:\docs\march**

This new MOVE command works only at the command line, though. See the DOS Commands chapter for more details about it. Let's go back to the Shell to see how to copy files.

TIP— *If you turned on Select Across Directories and forgot that it was on, you may find that you've got a whole bunch of files selected when you go to copy or move. Press Ctrl-\ to deselect all of them; then go back and select the one you want to work with. And turn off that pesky Select Across Directories unless you really want to do that.*

WARNING— *MOVE doesn't warn you about replacing files that already have the same name. For example, if you move memo.txt c:\docs.and there's already a MEMO. TXT file in the DOCS directory, it'll be overwritten by the MEMO.TXT file you're moving. And you can't get a file that's been overwritten back with the UNDELETE command!*

## Copying Files

Copying files with the mouse is easy, too. Just press Ctrl and drag the file into the folder where you want to copy it.

To copy more than one file, Shift-click to select adjacent files or Ctrl-click to select files that aren't next to each other. If you're copying groups of files by using the keyboard, press Shift-F8 to turn on Add mode and use the space bar to select the ones you want. Remember to turn on Select Across Directories on the Options menu if you want to copy files that are in more than one directory.

The advantage to using the Copy command (or F8) instead of dragging file icons is that you can use wildcards to speed up the copying process if you're copying files that have similar names. Suppose you want to copy everything ending in .WKS. You can just put *.WKS in the Copy dialog box. To copy every file beginning with A in the current directory, you'd enter A*.* To copy both the files named BROWN.TXT and BRAUN.TXT, you could enter BR??N.TXT.

> **TIP**— In the Shell, the keyboard shortcut for Copy is F8 and for Move is F7.

> **TIP**— Keep Confirm on Replace checked in the Confirmation options box so that you don't copy one file over another one that has the same name.

## Copying a File and Renaming It, Too

If you want your new copy to have a different name, use the keyboard to copy it. Then just enter its new name at the end of the path. For example, if you wanted to copy the file 3270.TXT into the directory C:\WINDOWS but name the copy NEW.TXT, you'd enter it like this:

> **TIP**— This is how to make a copy of a file in the same directory.

```
┌──────────────────────────────────────────────┐
│                  Copy File                     │
│                                                │
│                                                │
│   From:    3270.TXT                            │
│   To:      c:\windows\new.txt                  │
│                                                │
│                                                │
│                                                │
└──────────────────────────────────────────────┘
```

Of course, you can copy files at the command line, too. DOS has two of those commands, COPY and XCOPY, for copying files, as well as DISKCOPY for copying entire disks full of files. Look them up in Chapter 11, "DOS Commands," to see all sorts of examples.

## Copying Directories

Here's a tip for copying entire directories in the Shell. To copy all the files in one directory into another directory, choose the directory you want to copy. Then choose Select All from the File menu (or press Ctrl-/). Choose Copy; then type the path to the directory where you want to copy all the files and press Enter (or click OK). If the directory doesn't exist, you'll need to create it first.

**TIP—** *You can copy directories in the Shell or use the XCOPY command at the command line.*

# Plan Ahead

Whatever filing system you use, be sure to allow for future expansion. Files, like coat hangers, have a way of multiplying when you're not looking. If you have a directory structure with too many subdirectory levels, it'll soon get awkward to move between them, because there'll be so many different levels. Three subdirectories under a directory is about the limit. Beyond that, it starts getting irritating to move through a bunch of subdirectories to find the files you want to work with.

# Keyboard Shortcuts for Selecting Directories in the Shell

| | |
|---|---|
| **Select a directory** | Up and down arrow |
| **Select the root directory** | Home |
| **Select the last directory** | End |

# Keyboard Shortcuts for Expanding and Collapsing Directories in the Shell

| | |
|---|---|
| **Expand a selected directory one level** | + |
| **Expand a branch** | * |
| **Expand all** | Ctrl-* |
| **Collapse a directory** | – |

# Here's How To...

| | |
|---|---|
| **Change the current directory and see what's in it** | Click on it or move to it with the arrow keys (or use the DOS CD and DIR commands) |
| **See directories on another drive** | Select its disk drive icon or press Ctrl and type the drive letter (or use the DIR command and specify a drive) |
| **Reread a disk** | Double-click on the drive icon |
| **See into two directories at once** | Choose Dual File Lists from the View menu |
| **Sort a directory listing** | Choose File Display Options from the Options menu |
| **Look at groups of files with similar names in a directory** | Choose File Display Options and enter a wildcard pattern |
| **Create a directory** | Choose Create Directory from the File menu (or use the DOS MD command) |
| **Go to the root directory in the directory tree window** | Press Home |
| **Remove a directory** | Select it and press Del (or use the DOS RD command). It has to be empty first. At the command line, use the DEL-TREE command. |

| | |
|---|---|
| **Move a directory** | Use the MOVE command at the command line |
| **Move files** | Select them and drag them, or press F7, or choose Move from the File menu. At the command line, use the MOVE command. |
| **Copy files** | Select them and Ctrl-drag them, or press F8, or choose Copy from the File menu (or use the command-line COPY or XCOPY commands) |
| **Copy a file and rename it** | Press F8 and enter the new name at the end of the path |
| **Copy directories** | Select all the files in it and press F8; then type the path to the new directory. At the command line, use XCOPY. |

**Memory is the thing you forget with.**
—ALEXANDER CHASE, *Perspectives*, 1966

# Disks

Everything you do with your computer is either stored on floppy or hard disks or in ROM or put into your computer via a floppy disk (unless you're on a network or using a modem). So disks are very important. If you don't treat them right, your computer won't work right.

## Big Floppy Disks

If you're using 5.25-inch disks, take one out and look at it. It has a right side and a wrong side. The right side is the smooth one, and the wrong side has seams. You always want to put disks into your disk drive with the right side up and the oval cutout going into the drive first, pointing away from you. And remember to close the drive door when the disk is all the way in.

On one side of the disk there'll usually be a little square cutout. This is called the **write-protect notch** because when it's covered over, whatever's on the disk can't be changed, or written on. There may be a tab over the notch that you can remove. Once the tab's removed, you can change whatever's on the disk. If there isn't any notch, that disk is permanently write-protected.

> **TIP**— It's a good idea to keep your program disks—those that you buy—write-protected so that you don't ever change what's on any of them.

# Little Floppy Disks

If you're using 3.5-inch disks, they look a lot different from the 5.25-inch kind. The right side on them just shows a rectangular metal shutter. The wrong side has a round metallic insert in the middle. You put this kind of disk into the drive with the metal shutter going in first and the right side up. The drive door for this kind of disk will automatically close when the disk is in far enough.

On the top (right) side of the disk there'll be a square hole. This is the **write-protect tab.** If it's closed, you can change whatever's on the disk. If it's open, you can't. There's a slider on the back of the disk that lets you open and close this tab. Isn't it annoying that the computer world is so inconsistent? This is just the opposite of the way write protection works on the 5.25-inch floppy disks.

# Labels

Make labels for your floppy disks so that you can tell what's on them. Use a felt-tip pen, because pressing down with a pencil or a ballpoint pen can damage the delicate surface of the disk. Don't cover the notch (on 5.25-inch disks) with the label if you want to be able to change what's on the disk. Don't cover the oval cutout or the metal shutter (on 3.5-inch disks) with the label. Don't touch the part of the disk that you can see in the oval or round cutouts.

**TIP—** *The high-density 3.5-inch disks have two square holes! That's how you can tell them from the 720K disks. To tell a high-density 5.25-inch disk from a double-density disk, look for a hub ruing around the round hole. The 360K disks have one; the 1.2 Mb disks don't.*

# Disk Capacities

You'll hear disks talked about in terms of their capacity. "Is that a 360K disk, or is it 1.2 meg?" As you saw in Chapter 1, K stands for kilobyte, which is 1024 bytes. Meg is short for megabyte (Mb), which is a thousand kilobytes (a little over a million bytes). Here's a table that will take some of the mystery out of the jargon:

| Size | Capacity | In bytes, that's | Also called |
|------|----------|------------------|-------------|
| 5.25 | 360K | 368,640 | Double density |
| 5.25 | 1.2 Mb | 1,228,800 | High density |
| 3.5 | 720K | 737,280 | Double density |
| 3.5 | 1.44 Mb | 1,474,560 | High density |

Which kind of disk should you use? Well, you can't use the high-density disks unless you have a high-density disk drive, and you can't use the 3.5-inch disks unless you have a 3.5-inch disk drive, so that narrows your choices.

If you have a high-density disk drive, use high-density disks for your backups: they're more expensive, but you can put lots more files on them and keep the number of floppy disks you have to store to a minimum. If you're planning to swap disks with other people, who may not be so lucky as to have a high-density drive, though, better use the 360K disks, which almost everybody can accept (except those of you with PS/2s or laptops).

> **TIP**— A disk's sleeve is a paper cover that you store the disk in to keep dust out of it. When you read "take the disk out of its sleeve," that's referring to this paper envelope, not to the plastic cover that the disk is sealed in! The smaller 3.5-inch disks don't have sleeves because the shutter automatically closes to keep out dust.

## Compressing Floppy Disks for More Real Estate

DOS 6 comes with a new DoubleSpace utility that can compress floppy disks, which increases their capacity tremendously. A compressed disk can hold two or three times as many files as an uncompressed one. (DOS 6 can also compress your hard disk, which you should have done when you installed it—see the Appendix for how to do it if you didn't). When you compress a floppy disk that already has lots of files on it, it will hold lots more files. You can use them almost exactly as before, except that they'll hold much, much more. Here's how to do it:

> **WARNING**— If you're planning to exchange disks with other people who may not have DOS 6 and DoubleSpace, don't compress your floppies. Once a disk is compressed, it needs DoubleSpace to read it.

The disk you're planning to compress should be one that you've been using—one that's, say, about three-quarters full. You'll need about .65 Mb of free space on it. So you can't compress 360K 5.25-inch disks, because they're too small to begin with.

Put the disk in your floppy drive and start DoubleSpace by typing **dblspace** at the DOS prompt. Choose Existing Drive from the Compress menu, pick the drive the floppy's in, and type **c** for Compress. Then wait while the disk gets compressed.

DoubleSpace will compress the disk while you wait. That's the easy part. It's just a little trickier to *use* a compressed floppy disk (with a compressed hard disk, you don't have to fool with the rest of this stuff).

To use a compressed floppy, you have to "mount" the disk first. "Mounting" simply means using a command that lets DOS read what's on the disk. Say that you've compressed a disk that has files on it you want to keep for long-term storage, and now the time has come to take that disk out of mothballs and get a file or two off it. Put the disk in drive A (or B) and type **dblspace /mount a:** (or b:) at the DOS prompt. You'll see a message when the disk is mounted, and then you can use it just as you would a regular disk.

> **TIP**— You'll see a message that "drive" A (or B) will be compressed and that once a drive is compressed, it can't be uncompressed. It's OK. Just the disk in the drive will be compressed. You can keep on using regular floppy disks in that drive, too.

> **TIP**— If you plan to use compressed floppy disks a lot, put a dblspace /mount a: (or b:) line in your AUTOEXEC.BAT file so that DOS will mount the disk each time you start your computer. See Chapter 10 for how to edit your AUTOEXEC.BAT.

# Formatting Disks

Before you can use a disk, DOS has to prepare it so that it can read it. This is called **formatting** (on a Mac, it's called initializing. Same thing).

Usually, when you buy a box of disks, they're not formatted. (You can buy preformatted disks, but they're sort of expensive.) But there'll probably be times when you're looking at a blank, unlabeled disk, wondering whether it's ready to use or not. How can you tell whether a disk needs to be formatted? Easy. Put it in the drive and try to get a directory listing of what's on it. (In the Shell, click on the drive icon, or highlight

> **TIP**— When you format a disk, everything that's on it is wiped out. You can get it back, though, with the UNFORMAT and REBUILD commands. They're discussed in the DOS Commands section of this book, Chapter 11.

```
┌──┤ Show Information ├──┐
│                        │
│ File                   │
│   Name  : 483CH2.REV   │
│   Attr  : ...a         │
│ Selected      A    C   │
│   Number:     1    1   │
│   Size  :      73,508  │
│ Directory              │
│   Name  : CH2          │
│   Size  :      88,800  │
│   Files :          11  │
│ Disk                   │
│   Name  : none         │
│   Size  :   1,213,952  │
│   Avail :       1,024  │
│   Files :         121  │
│   Dirs  :          12  │
│                        │
│ (_Close )    ( Help )  │
└────────────────────────┘
```

it and press Enter.) If you get the sort of scary message "General failure," don't panic. It just means that the disk in drive A hasn't been formatted yet, not that your computer has generally failed. Choose Cancel to cancel the command; then go ahead and format the disk.

If you get a list of files that are on the disk, it's already been formatted. If there's any space available on it, you can use it for storing more files. To see how much space is available, highlight the disk drive icon, choose Show Information from the Options menu, and check out what's next to "Avail." If you're running the DIR command, you'll see a number of "bytes free" at the bottom of the listing. You can delete files you don't want to free more space.

## *Formatting a Floppy Disk*

OK, you've got a brand-new floppy disk. Here's how to format it in the Shell:

1. Choose Format from the Disk Utilities menu (you can double-click on the Disk Utilities icon if you have a mouse). You'll see a dialog box asking you for parameters. If you want to format the disk as a system disk, or format it in a different capacity, you'd enter some cryptic options here (they'll be discussed later in this chapter).

2. Just press Enter to format what's in drive A. If you want to format a disk in drive B, type *b:* and press Enter.

3. You'll be prompted to insert the disk and press Enter. When you do, DOS will go ahead and format it. It'll tell you what capacity it's formatting the disk in and how it's doing.

**TIP**— *Check to see that nothing's on a disk (or that there's nothing there that you want to keep) before you format it. To do this in the Shell, click on the icon of the disk drive, or highlight it and press Enter. With the command line, get a directory listing with the DIR command.*

```
┌──────────────────────┤ Format ├─────────────────────┐
│ Enter the drive to format.                           │
│                                                      │
│ Parameters . . .    ┌──────────────────────────────┐ │
│                     │a:_                            │ │
│                     └──────────────────────────────┘ │
│      ( OK )            ( Cancel )          ( Help )  │
└──────────────────────────────────────────────────────┘
```

When it's done, it'll ask you if you want to format another disk. Type either Y or N and press Enter. If it's N, press any key to get back to the Shell, if you started out from there.

## Quick Formatting

If a disk has already been formatted and has files on it, you can do a quick format on it in the Shell. Choose Quick Format from the Disk Utilities menu instead of Format. This will clean off everything on the disk very quickly. It's a lot faster than doing a regular format.

> TIP— Use Quick Format on used disks.

Instead of using the Disk Utilities menu, you can also use the FORMAT command by running it from the File menu or the command line. Enter the command like this: FORMAT A: or FORMAT B: and press Enter. Be sure to tell DOS which drive the disk is in, or it'll tell you that you have to specify a drive letter.

> TIP— Don't format C: or D: unless you're really formatting your hard disk! DOS will warn you if you try to do this.

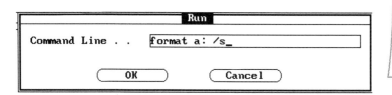

```
┌──────────────────────────┤ Run ├────────────────────┐
│                                                      │
│ Command Line . .    ┌──────────────────────────────┐ │
│                     │format a: /s_                  │ │
│                     └──────────────────────────────┘ │
│           ( OK )                ( Cancel )           │
└──────────────────────────────────────────────────────┘
```

When the formatting's done, you'll be asked if you want to give the disk a label.

## Using a Label

You can give disks an electronic label of as many as 11 characters. You can use spaces here, so your disk labels can be more meaningful than file names! It's OK not to give a newly formatted disk a label. But you may want to label them to identify their owner (you) or to indicate what kinds of files are stored on the disk, like OCT REPORTS. It's up to you.

## Doing the Job

Formatting disks is a dull, time-consuming job. You should probably put on some of your favorite music and sit there and format as many disks as you can stand, just so you'll have a good supply handy. Formatting disks gets rather mechanical after a while.

Put a (real) label on the disks that have been formatted so that you don't waste time formatting them again! I put a blank label on the ones I've formatted. If they already have labels, you can put a tiny check in the corner, just something that tells you "I've been formatted."

### FORMATTING DISKS IN DIFFERENT CAPACITIES

DOS knows what kind of disk drives you have, and it will format the disks you put in them accordingly. However, you may sometimes want to format a 360K (double-density) disk in a high-density (1.2 Mb) disk drive, so that you can exchange it with other folks who may not have a high-density drive. You can do that by giving the FORMAT command as **format a: /f:360**. (You can either use the Disk Utilities' Format command or run the FORMAT command at the command line.)

You can also format 720K (double-density) disks in 1.44 Mb (3.5-inch) drives. To do that, give the FORMAT command as **format b: /f:720**. (Use the letter of the drive you're using.)

Whatever you do, don't try to format a 360K or 720K disk as a high-density disk. And don't try to format a high-density disk as a double-density disk. It may look like the formatting has been done, but you'll find later that it may cause problems. To tell them apart, remember that high-density 3.5-inch disks have two square holes. And high-density 5.25-inch disks don't have a hub ring around their round hole. If you have a high-density disk drive, use the f:/360 or f:/720 switches just described to format double-density disks in that drive.

# Formatting a System Disk

You can also format a disk with the DOS system files on it so that you can use it to start your computer, if you have to, without using your hard disk. Normally, you don't need to put the system files on disks you format, because you just use them for storing data, not starting your computer. If you put a disk that has system files in drive A and restart the computer, DOS will start from it, bypassing your hard disk.

> **TIP—** *You can use the Uninstall disk you created when you installed DOS 6 as an emergency startup disk.*

Once your computer has started again, you can use this disk, if you have to, to reformat your hard disk and restore your backed-up files onto it.

```
┌─────────────────────────────────────────────────┐
│                      Run                          │
│                                                   │
│  Command Line  . .   format a: /s_                │
│                                                   │
│           ┌──────────┐      ┌──────────┐          │
│           │    OK    │      │  Cancel  │          │
│           └──────────┘      └──────────┘          │
└─────────────────────────────────────────────────┘
```

To format a disk with the DOS system files on it, just give an extra /S option to the FORMAT command. For a disk in drive A, you'd use FORMAT A: /S, for example.

Once you've got the system files and COMMAND.COM on the disk, that's really all you need to run DOS from that floppy disk. It's a good idea, though, to also copy from your DOS directory CHKDSK.EXE (so that you can check the hard disk), FORMAT.COM (in case you have to reformat the hard disk), and BACKUP.EXE and RESTORE.EXE (in case you can salvage some files from the hard disk). Label the disk "emergency disk" and keep it in a safe place. Then, if your hard disk fails, and your Uninstall disk isn't to be found, you can restart your computer with this disk in drive A.

> **TIP—** *If you're using a disk that's already been formatted, you can just run the SYS command to put the system files on it. SYS B:. for example, puts the system files on a formatted disk in drive B.*

After your computer's restarted, you can use one of the special utility programs like the Norton Utilities, if you have it, to see what happened to your hard disk and perhaps repair it.

For example, at the A> prompt, you can use the CHKDSK command to inspect your hard disk (the kind of information this command gives is explained in the DOS commands section). If you get a message that there are an enormous number of bad sectors, you can reformat it.

# Formatting a Hard Disk

Let's all hope that you never have to do this, because formatting wipes out everything on your hard disk, but the day may come. You may start to get serious error messages about your hard disk, or you may have bought a new hard disk that hasn't been formatted yet.

> **TIP**—Don't do this unless you have to! If you have to, you'll know. Nothing will be working right.

If you have to format a hard disk that's not working right, here's how to do it. First, turn your computer off, put a DOS disk (either the Uninstall disk or the disk labeled "emergency" that you made) in drive A, and turn it on again. Tell DOS the date and time if it asks.

You'll see an A:\> prompt, because the computer has started from drive A instead of drive C this time. At the prompt, type *format c: /s* and press Enter. (This will put the system files on your hard disk.) You'll then be prompted about whether this is really what you want to do. After the formatting is done, you'll be asked for a volume label. You can give your hard disk a name of up to 11 characters, including spaces. You might want to call it "Drive C," or use your name or, after what you've been through, name it "Titanic." Or use no label at all.

If you get error messages when you try to format the disk, there's probably more wrong with it than you want to deal with. Call your dealer or a guru.

If you're formatting a brand-new hard disk right out of the box, there are a couple of other things you may need to do. First, you need to check if low-level formatting has been done on the disk (they usually come with this done to them, or it may be done automatically the first time you start the computer). If not, check to see if any additional instructions came with the disk, and follow them. Then you can run the Setup program to install DOS (see the appendix) and it will format your hard disk.

# Here's How To...

| | |
|---|---|
| **Protect a 5.25" disk** | Cover the write-protect notch |
| **Protect a 3.5" disk** | Uncover the write-protect notch |
| **Format a disk** | Choose Format from the Disk Utilities group, or use the DOS FORMAT command |
| **See how much space is available on a disk** | Choose Show Information from the Options menu, or use the DIR or CHKDSK commands |
| **Do a quick format on a used disk to free space on it** | Choose Quick Format from the Disk Utilities group or use the FORMAT /Q command |
| **Format a 360K 5.25" disk in a high-density drive** | Give the options as A: /F:360 (use the letter of your drive) |
| **Format a 720K 3.5" disk in a high-density drive** | Give the options as B: /F:720 (use the letter of your drive) |
| **Make a startup disk** | Use the /S switch with the Format command on a disk that's being formatted, or use the DOS SYS command on a disk that's already formatted |

**73**

> **Put all your eggs in one basket and—watch that basket.**
>
> —MARK TWAIN, *Pudd'nhead Wilson's Calendar*, 1894

# Programs

Starting with DOS 5, you can have several programs in memory at once and switch between them almost instantly. You can be running a word processing program and switch over to your spreadsheet to check a few facts and dates, or you can look up someone's name and address in your database quickly. How many programs you can run depends on how much memory you have, but I've run WordPerfect and Lotus 1-2-3 at the same time on a plain old IBM XT with no problem at all.

When you first start the Shell, the screen shows only the Main group of programs—Command Prompt, Editor, QBasic, and the Disk Utilities. You can add programs to this group and create new groups of your own. This chapter will show you how to do that, and it will also show you some new ways to start programs.

## *Running Programs*

You can run programs in several different ways with DOS 6:

- By choosing Run from the File menu and entering the command used to start the program

● By going out to the DOS command prompt (press Shift-F9 or choose Command Prompt from the Main group) and starting the program as you normally would

● By selecting a program from the file list (you can just double-click on it with a mouse)

● By selecting a program item from a program group (double-click on it, too)

● By selecting a program file or a document that's been "associated" with a program (you'll see how to do that in this chapter).

## Using the Run Command

The File menu's Run command lets you start a program from within the Shell. Just enter the command you use to start the program in the Run dialog box. For example, to run Microsoft Word, you'd just enter *word* in the Run dialog box and choose OK.

**TIP**— *This is a good way to run programs you don't use often.*

If you normally have to change to a specific directory to start the program, you'll need to enter the path to it. If you always had to change to the WORD directory to run Word, you'd enter C:\WORD\WORD, for example.

You can also run DOS commands by entering them in the Run dialog box. When you install DOS, the Setup program puts in your AUTOEXEC.BAT file the path to where these commands are stored. This is usually a directory called C:\DOS. So you could just enter *format a:* to format a disk in Drive A, for example.

**TIP**— *See Chapter 10 for how to put a program in your path so that you don't have to change directories to run it.*

## Using the DOS Command Prompt

You can also use the DOS command prompt to start programs. If you've used DOS before, this is the way you've always started them.

To use the DOS command prompt, choose it from the Main group, or press Shift-F9. When you're done with the command line, you can get back to the Shell by typing *exit*. To remove the Shell from memory, choose Exit from the File menu or press F3 or Alt-F4.

## Starting a Program by Choosing Its Name

You can start a program running just by choosing its name in the file list. Double-click on it with the mouse, or move the highlight to it with the arrow keys and press Enter. Programs always have an .EXE or .COM extension, and their icons are different from document icons (documents are dog-eared, with one corner turned down).

```
CONFIG   .SYS
DUMP     .BAT
```

You can start a program that's in a program group just by double-clicking on its name (or highlighting its name and pressing Enter, if you haven't got a mouse). For example, to use the Backup program in the Disk Utilities group, open the group and choose Backup Fixed Disk.

### REFRESHING AND REPAINTING THE SCREEN

*If you're running a special kind of program called a* **pop-up program,** *(also sometimes called a TSR), you may need to repaint the screen after you've quit the program, because it may still be visible. Repaint Screen is on the View menu, and its shortcut is Shift-F5.*

*Sometimes you may need to refresh the screen display, too. For example, if you've created new files or deleted old ones in a word processing program, the screen may not reflect the changes. Pressing F5 will update the screen, or you can choose Refresh from the View menu. When you refresh the screen, your hard disk is read all over again and you go back to the root directory. Very annoying.*

If a document's been associated with a program, you can choose its name to open it and start the program running. You'll see how to associate documents and programs later in this chapter.

# Using the Task Swapper

The Task Swapper is the neat feature that lets you switch between programs that you've started running. To use it, choose Enable Task Swapper from the Options menu. You'll see a small black symbol next to Task Swapper when it's on.

Then start the programs you want to switch among. In the file list or program list, double-click on the program you want to add or highlight it and press Shift-Enter. As soon as the program starts, press Ctrl-Esc to get back to the Shell. Then start the next program you want to be able to switch to. After you start each one, it'll be listed in a new area of the Shell screen called the active task list.

Once the programs are listed in the active task list, you can double-click on it to switch to it or move to it with the arrow keys and press Enter, if you don't have a mouse.

While you're in a program and you've got several running, you can hold down the Alt key and press Tab to see the name of the next program in the active task list. Release Alt when you see the name of the one you want to switch to.

When you exit from the program, its name is removed from the active task list. You'll need to exit from all the programs you have running before you can exit from the Shell, or you'll get rebuked with a dialog box.

If a program hangs up on you, go to the Shell (press Ctrl-Esc) highlight its name in the active task list, and delete it. To be on the safe side, restart your computer, just in case there might be problems with the unexpected exit.

**TIP—** *To cycle between all the programs you've got running, hold down Alt and press Tab again and again. To return to the Shell, press Ctrl-Esc.*

**TIP—** *Sometimes you may be asked to press Ctrl-C to exit from a special kind of program called a pop-up program. Then just press any key to get back to the Shell.*

## Returning to the Shell from Windows

Windows runs beautifully under DOS 6; it's thankful for all that extra memory. But you can't return to the Shell with Ctrl-Esc from Windows, because that key combination brings up the Task List in Windows. To return to the Shell from Windows, exit from Windows and then press any key.

# Setting Up Program Groups

You can set up groups of your own so that they'll appear in the program list in the Shell. For example, you might like to organize your work by project or by client and keep all the programs and documents you work with every day in each group. Or if you work with several graphics programs, you might put them all in one group so that you can find them easily. You can have a copy of a program in as many groups as you like; putting a program in a group just gives you a new way to start it. It doesn't really make another copy of it that eats up room on your hard disk.

> **TIP**—*Just because you put a program or a document into a group doesn't mean that you have to always start it from the group. You can still start it just as you've always done.*

To use an item in a group, double-click on the group's name to open the group (or use the arrow keys and Enter). You can then choose an item from that group. To close a program group, do the same thing.

## Creating a Group

To create a group of your own, first display the group you want to add the new group to. For instance, if it's to go in the Main group, display the Main group. (Have the highlight on

> **TIP**—*You need to be looking at the Program/File List or the Program List view to create a new group.*

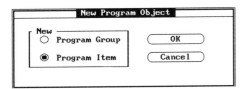

Command Prompt, Editor, or MS-DOS Qbasic.) Then choose New from the File menu. You'll see a dialog box; select Program Group and then OK.

You'll then see the Add Group dialog box. In this one, type the name you want your new group to have. You can use spaces and as many as 23 characters. Press Tab to move to the next line.

TIP— You can also add a Help message (up to 255 characters) about what the group is for. If you're setting up groups for others, this might be a good idea.

```
┌──────────────Add Group──────────────┐
│ Required                            │
│   Title . . . .  ┌Johnson Project_┐ │
│                  └────────────────┘ │
│ Optional                            │
│   Help Text . .  ┌────────────────┐ │
│                  └────────────────┘ │
│   Password  . .  ┌──────────┐       │
│                  └──────────┘       │
└─────────────────────────────────────┘
```

You can also assign a password to your new group. If you're sharing a computer with others, this is a way of getting privacy: no one can open your group except those who know the password. (Anybody can run a program from the DOS prompt, though.)

TIP— Better write that password down in a secret place somewhere because "paper remembers so that you can forget."

```
┌──────────────Main──────────────┐
│ ▭  Command Prompt              │
│ ▭  Editor                      │
│ ▭  MS-DOS QBasic               │
│ ▦  Disk Utilities              │
│ ▦  Johnson Project             │
└────────────────────────────────┘
```

When you've set your group up, choose OK. You'll see the group's name and an icon for it (if you're using a graphics display) appear in the program list.

If you decide later that you want to change the group name, choose Properties from the File menu. You can change the name, the password, and the Help message, if there's one. (You have to know the original password, though.)

## Adding Items

Now you've got a new, empty group, so the next step is to add items to it. They can be either programs or documents. Say you want to add WordPerfect to a group. Highlight the group name and open it. Then choose New from the File menu. This time, click Program Item if it's not already selected.

**TIP**— *Make sure the name of the group you want to add the item to is at the top of the program list.*

```
┌──────────────────── Add Program ─────────────────────┐
│                                                       │
│  Program Title . . . . [WordPerfect_____]   │
│                                                       │
│  Commands   . . . . . . [wp_____]   │
│                                                       │
│  Startup Directory . . [_____]    │
│                                                       │
│  Application Shortcut Key  [ALT+W_____]   │
│                                                       │
│  [X] Pause after exit      Password . .  [_____]   │
│                                                       │
│      ( OK )    ( Cancel )    ( Help )   ( Advanced... )│
│                                                       │
└───────────────────────────────────────────────────────┘
```

Type the name that you want to appear in the group in the Program Title box. It doesn't have to be the real name of the program; you can use something more descriptive. In the Commands box, type the *exact command* you use to start the program. If you normally start WordPerfect with the WP command, type *wp*.

If you want to change to a different directory when you start the program, type the path to that directory in the Startup Directory box. Suppose, for example, that you keep Microsoft Word in a directory named C:\WORD but you want to make the C:\WORD\DOCS directory current when you start Word so that you save all your documents there. In this case you'd type C:\WORD\DOCS in the Startup Directory box.

If you want to be able to switch to the program with a special shortcut key sequence, use the Application Shortcut Key box. Once you've assigned a shortcut key, pressing that key sequence switches you to the program directory once it's running and displayed in the active task list. You won't have to press Alt-Tab to cycle through your running programs or choose the program's name from the active task list.

The shortcut key you select has to be either a Shift, Alt, or Ctrl key combination. If a combination's already been used, DOS won't let you have it as a shortcut key. For example, Alt-F opens the File menu, so you can't use that. You might want to choose Ctrl-W for WordPerfect, just something that's easy to remember.

**TIP—** *Check out Help to see a list of combinations that are already taken.*

Keep Pause After Exit checked if you want to be able to return to the Shell when you exit from the program.

You can also enter a password. If you do, you'll be prompted for it before DOS will start the program.

When you're done, choose OK.

Now here's a neat trick. You can add documents to program groups, too. The trick is to give the document's name as the "Program Title" (you can use a description here, too) and then enter the path to the document in the Commands box, putting the command used to start the program first. If you forget the program command, the document won't open.

**TIP—** *You can add documents to your groups, too.*

```
┌─────────────────── Add Program ───────────────────┐
│                                                    │
│  Program Title . . . .  ┌Floor Plan──────────────┐ │
│                         └────────────────────────┘ │
│  Commands   . . . . . . ┌wp c:\wp51\ch2_─────────┐ │
│                         └────────────────────────┘ │
│  Startup Directory . .  ┌────────────────────────┐ │
│                         └────────────────────────┘ │
│  Application Shortcut Key  ┌──────────────────────┐│
│                           └──────────────────────┘ │
│  [X] Pause after exit      Password . .  ┌────────┐│
│                                          └────────┘│
│      ╭────╮    ╭──────╮    ╭──────╮   ╭──────────╮ │
│      │ OK │    │Cancel│    │ Help │   │Advanced..│ │
│      ╰────╯    ╰──────╯    ╰──────╯   ╰──────────╯ │
└────────────────────────────────────────────────────┘
```

Here WordPerfect will open the document named CH2 when you click on Floor Plan.

**TIP—** *Main's always listed so that you can get back to it.*

## Copying Program Items

A quick way to get programs and documents into the groups you create is to copy them from groups that you've already set up. To do this, just open the group that already has the program in it; then select the program you want to copy. Then choose Copy from the File menu and open the group you want to copy the program into. To complete the copy, press F2. Unfortunately, you can't drag with the mouse or use the F8 keyboard shortcut to copy program items.

Remember, you can have several copies of a program or document in different groups. Choosing Copy doesn't really create a new copy of the program on your hard disk; it just gives you a new way to run it.

**TIP**— *Use the Reorder command to reorder the items in a group and put the ones you use most often at the top. Select the item; choose Reorder; then select the new location and press Enter or double-click.*

## Deleting Programs and Groups

You can delete a program from a group by highlighting it and pressing Del. If a password's been assigned, you'll need to know it to delete the program.

To delete a group, delete all the items in it first; then delete the group.

**TIP**— *This doesn't delete the program from your hard disk.*

## Associating Files

One other neat thing you can do is to associate documents with the programs that "own" them. After a document's been associated with a program, double-clicking on its name or choosing it with the keyboard starts the program and opens the document at the same time.

When you associate documents, you tell DOS that all the files ending in a certain extension are associated with a certain program.

For example, to associate all the files that end in .IGF with the program HiJaak, you'd highlight one of the .IGF files and then choose Associate from the File menu. When the dialog box

**WARNING**— *If you've chosen Select Across Directories, you may not see the extension you want in the Associate dialog box. Go back and Deselect All (Ctrl-\).*

comes up, fill it out with the command used to start the program, in this case hj.exe.

An alternate way to do it is to highlight the program, choose Associate, and in the dialog box type in all the different extensions you want to associate with it, separating each one with a space. This is a faster way if you're associating more than one extension with a program.

# Viewing Program Groups

The very first time you start the Shell, you see the Program/File Lists. You can choose Program List to see just program groups and the active task list. If you've running a lot of programs at once, this may be the view you'd like to see instead of all the files and directories.

TIP— *DOS remembers what view you looked at last and shows that view to you the next time you start your computer.*

# Here's How To...

| | |
|---|---|
| **Run a program** | Choose Run from the File menu or go to the DOS prompt and enter the command you normally use; select the program from the file list; or select a document that's associated with a program; or select the program from a group |
| **Use the DOS prompt** | Press Shift-F9 or choose Command Prompt from the Main group |
| **Exit to DOS** | Press F3 or Alt-F4 or choose Exit from the File menu |
| **Run several programs** | Choose Enable Task Swapper from the Options menu; start the programs |
| **Cycle among programs** | Press Alt-Tab or choose a program's name from the active task list |
| **Switch from a program to the active task list** | Press Ctrl-Esc |
| **Create a group** | Open the group you want to add the new group to (usually Main); choose New from the File menu; select Program Group |

| | |
|---|---|
| **Change a group's name, password, or Help screen** | Highlight the group; choose Properties from the File menu |
| **Open a program group** | Highlight it and press Enter or double-click on it |
| **Add a program to a group** | Highlight the group; choose New from the File menu; select Program Item |
| **Add a document to a group** | Same as adding a program, but fill out the Command box with the command used to start the program, followed by the path to the document |
| **Copy a program item into a group** | Select the program you want to copy; choose Copy from the File menu; open the group you want to copy the program into; press F2 |
| **Delete a program item from a group** | Highlight the item's name in the group; press Del |
| **Delete a group** | Delete all the program items in it first |
| **Associate files and programs** | Highlight a file that has the extension you want to associate or highlight the program; choose Associate from the File menu |
| **View just programs** | Choose Program List from the View menu |

**8**

**A good scare is worth more than good advice.**
—EDGAR WATSON HOWE, *Country Town Sayings*, 1911

# DOS 6's Neat New Utilities

Sooner or later, something will go wrong with your computer or your disks. Not "may," *will*. Also, there's the possibility of human error: you may accidentally erase a directory full of files you wanted to keep and not find out until several days later that that's what you did. And, in today's global village, there's always the possibility that your computer can catch a virus from a floppy disk you put into it or from a file you download. To protect your work, you need to make backups— copies of all the work you do and all the programs you've bought. You need to be able to delete files you deleted by mistake, and you need a good virus-protection program. DOS 6 comes with all three of these utilities, both in DOS and Windows versions (see the Appendix for how to install DOS 6 or how to go back and install these utilities later, if you didn't install them during setup).

In this chapter, we'll look at Microsoft Backup, Undelete, and Anti-Virus. But first we'll look at some tips for working safely.

# Working Safely

You don't *have* to use DOS 6's new Microsoft Backup utility or purchase a fancy backup utility program to make duplicate copies of your work. You can just make disk copies of all your program disks and copies of all your important documents; this is what I do.

Purists say make two copies, in addition to what's on your hard disk. Why? Consider this scenario. The file on your hard disk isn't working right, so you get out your backup copy and put it in your disk drive. What's wrong, though, is really with your disk drive, and it eats your backup copy. At this point you realize what's happening, but it's too late: your data's lost. If you have another backup copy, you still have your data. You can get your hard disk repaired and you'll still have your work.

## What Are Backups?

Backups are *not* copies of the same file on the same disk. Backups are copies that are on a different disk or on another medium, such as magnetic tape, and that you store somewhere away from your computer. Then, if your office catches on fire or your computer "walks," your backups are somewhere else.

### IT CAN HAPPEN TO YOU, TOO

*No matter how careful you are, something can happen to ruin your work. This happened to me. I was working in WordPerfect when everything went wrong and I found myself out in DOS again. I called Word-Perfect Corporation, thinking it was the program that was at fault, and we had a long conversation about what I was doing (running a macro) and what had happened. They said (I've boiled the conversation down to its essence), "Cosmic ray." I called a fellow who was a DOS expert and told him what was going on and he said, "Cosmic ray." (Actually, he said my FAT was broken—I thought that sounded like a good thing at first—but he meant my file allocation table, which DOS uses to keep track of where everything is.) Nothing I did or didn't do caused this to happen; it just happened. Cosmic ray.*

There are several different ways to make backup copies.

- Choose Disk Copy from the Disk Utilities group in the Shell, or use the DISKCOPY command to make backup copies of entire floppy disks, like program disks that you buy or collections of clip art on disks.

- Choose Copy from the File menu in the Shell, or, at the command line use the COPY or XCOPY commands to copy just the files and directories that you want copies of.

- Use the Microsoft Backup utility at the command line (or in Windows) to back up a whole hard disk (take a "snapshot" of what's on it) or back up just selected directories.

We'll look at all of these.

# Backing Up a Program Disk

To make a backup copy of a program disk you've bought or an entire floppy disk of files, use the Disk Copy command in the Shell's Disk Utilities group or the DISKCOPY command.

## Using Disk Copy

When you double-click on Disk Copy (or highlight it with the arrow keys and press Enter, if you don't have a mouse), you'll see a dialog box all set up for you, assuming that you want to copy the disk in drive A onto a disk in drive B. If that's what you want, fine.

But what if you have only one disk drive? It's still OK. DOS will figure out that you have only one and will do the disk copy, prompting you to insert the original disk (called the **source disk**) and the one you're making the copy on (called the **destination disk**).

Your destination disk (the one that's going to be the new copy)

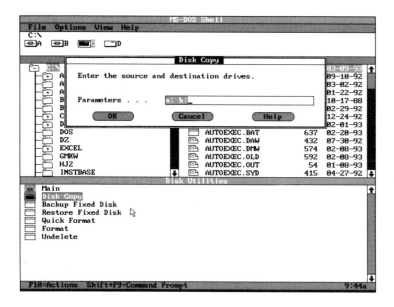

doesn't have to be formatted. You can use a new disk right out of the box. DOS will format it as it goes along.

When the disk copy is done (you'll be taken out to DOS for this part, just as though you were using the DOS DISKCOPY command), you'll be asked if you want to make more copies. After you're done copying disks, press any key to return to the Shell.

You can't copy copy-protected disks or the files on them. To copy them, get a program like COPY II PC from Central Point Software.

## Using the COPY Command

The second way to copy all the files on one disk onto another disk is to use the COPY command. It has two advantages: it lets you copy what's on a disk in drive A onto a disk in drive B even if they're different sizes, and it also reorganizes the copied files so that DOS can find them faster (they may have been scattered all over the original disk because of the way DOS stores files).

To copy all the files on one disk to another (assuming there aren't any subdirectories), if the original's in drive A and the copy's to be in drive B, click on the drive A icon, choose Select All from the File menu (or press Ctrl-/) and then press F8 and enter *b:* in the To: box.

Remember, if you only have one disk drive, don't worry: DOS will figure it out and prompt you to insert the disk that's going to be the copy.

# Using Microsoft Backup

If you don't maintain duplicate copies of your files, you'll probably want to use DOS 6's new Backup utility to back up your whole hard disk so you'll have a copy of everything that's on it. The new Backup utility (called Microsoft Backup or MSBACKUP for short) will also let you back up just selected directories. You were asked whether you wanted to install it (for DOS, for Windows, or for both) when you installed DOS 6. If you didn't install it then, you can go back and do it now (see the Appendix for how).

> **TIP**— It's a good idea to organize your filing system so that you keep data files directories separate from program files. That way, you can just back up your data directories.

The strategy you use for backups (see the sidebar "Different Kinds of Backups")and how often you make a backup depends on what you do. If you're working on your computer for several hours every day, you'll probably want to make daily backups. If you work only a couple of hours a week, make backups whenever you think you've done enough work that you don't want to lose.

## Making the Backup

To start MSBACKUP, type *msbackup* at the DOS prompt. The first time you run it, DOS 6 will do a compatibility test on your system. After it's done, you'll see a screen with Backup, Restore, Compare, Configure, and Quit buttons. Choose Backup, and you'll see the screen on the following page.

> **TIP**— MSBACKUP will figure out how many floppy disks you need and tell you before you start the backup. It can format disks as you go, too, so you don't need formatted floppies.

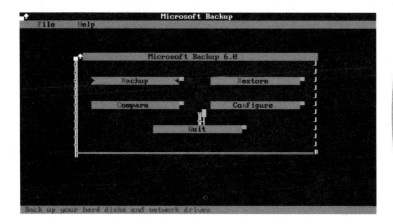

TIP— *If all you want to do is back up your entire drive C to floppies in drive A, everything's already set up for you. Type msbackup, type b for Backup, and choose Start Backup by pressing Alt-S.*

In the Backup To box, choose the floppy drive you're going to use, and whether you'll be using high-density or double-density disks. In the Backup From box, choose the drive that

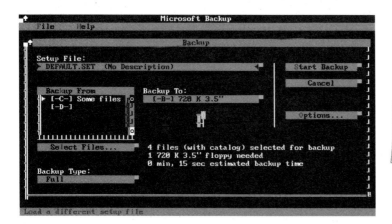

TIP— *Look back in Chapter 2 or get Help while you're in the backup utility if you need help using the keyboard and mouse to make choices from screens like this one.*

you're backing up from (usually drive C, your hard disk, so you won't need to change it). If you're not backing up the whole hard disk, choose Select Files. MSBACKUP will read your whole hard disk and show you all the files and directories on it.

Use the space bar or the *right* mouse button to select the directories and files that you want to back up. To select all the files in a directory, just press the space bar. If you only want to back up selected files, choose them by pressing the right arrow key or clicking with the mouse to move into the list of files. Then select the files you want with the space bar or right mouse button.

If you know that you want to include some types of files but not others, you can use the Include, Exclude, and Special buttons. For example, you might want to exclude program files (which end in .EXE or .COM). You can press F1 to get help about any of these options.

Choose OK when you've selected all the files you want, and you'll go back to the main screen, which will now display how many files you've selected, how many floppy disks you'll need, and roughly how much time the backup will take.

## Picking a Backup Strategy

There are two different types of backups: **incremental backups** and **differential backups**. When you do an incremental backup, you back up the files that have changed since the last time you did any kind of backup, whether it was a full backup (of everything) or an incremental backup. When you do a differential backup, you back up only the files that have been changed since the last full backup. Here are examples. You do a full backup on Day 1, backing up everything; then on Day 2, you do an incremental backup, backing up just the documents you

created or changed with on Day 2. On Day 3, you do another incremental backup, backing up just the files that you worked with on Day 3. You continue until, say, Day 10, when you do a full backup again and back up everything. That's how to use an incremental backup strategy.

For a differential backup strategy, you first do a full backup, say, on Friday. The next day, you back up all files that were changed on Monday. On Tuesday, you back up all files that were changed since Monday. On Wednesday, you back up all files that were changed since Monday. Friday rolls around, and you do a full backup again. That's a differential backup strategy.

Which to choose? If you regularly work with a lot of files, differential backups may take a little longer than incremental backups, because you're backing up everything that has changed since a certain day. But you won't have to maintain a whole lot of floppy disks, because you can alternate between two sets of disks, using one on Monday, one on Tuesday, the first on Wednesday, the second on Thursday, and so forth. The bottom line: Use a differential backup strategy if you find that you're using roughly the same set of files every day. Choose the incremental backup method if you usually work with different files every day.

Under Backup Type, choose Incremental or Differential if you're not doing a full backup (see the sidebar "Picking a Backup Strategy").

## Restoring Backed-Up Files

Let's hope you won't ever have to restore your backed-up files and that you keep them only for insurance. If you do have to restore them someday, here's how to do it.

Start backup by typing *msbackup* at the DOS prompt. Choose the Restore button, and you'll see this screen:

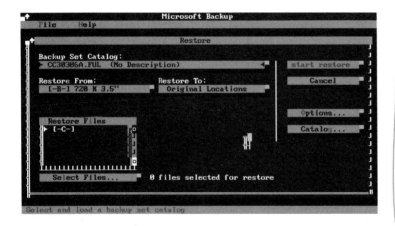

Go to the Backup Set Catalog box and pick the backup set you want to restore. DOS keeps information about each backup

> **TIP—** *MSBACKUP will let you restore files to a different location, so you can use it for transferring files between your desktop PC and a notebook computer.*

> **TIP—** *If you're restoring files that were backed up with a previous version of DOS using the BACKUP command, use the RESTORE command instead of Microsoft Backup. That BACKUP command is no longer part of DOS 6, but RESTORE is still there in case you need it.*

---

### READING A CATALOG'S NAME

(fyi) Consider this catalog name: CD31028A.FUL. The C is the first drive backed up (drive C) and the D is the last drive backed up on October 28, 1993 (the 3 represents the last digit of the year; the 10 is the month; and the 28 is the day). The A indicates that this was the first backup that day, and the .FUL indicates a full backup. An incremental backup ends in .INC, and a differential backup ends in .DIF.

you make in a catalog file that ends in .CAT (see the sidebars "Reading a Catalog's Name" and "Keep It Simple: Back Up Only What You Need").

In the Restore From box, choose the drive that has the backed-up files on it. If you're not restoring the files to their original locations, go to the Restore To box and choose the drive or directory you want to restore them to; then choose OK. Under Restore Files, if you're restoring all the files on the drive, click with the right mouse button on a drive letter or press the space bar. To select specific files or directories to restore, choose Select Files and select just those you want to restore. You can select whole directories with the right mouse button or the space bar. Choose OK, and you'll go back to the main screen, where you can choose Start Restore. You'll be prompted to insert disks as needed.

> **TIP—** *Always try to use high-density disks for backing up large numbers of files so you don't have to sit there and feed the computer as often.*

## KEEP IT SIMPLE: BACK UP ONLY WHAT YOU NEED

*Don't just automatically back up your whole hard disk every week. Once you have programs running the way you want them, you can back up the whole hard disk just once, if it makes you feel better and if you've done some tweaking to make everything work the way you want. Or you can just consider your program installation disks as your backup disks for program files.*

*What you really need to back up is your data files. But you don't have to back up all of them, either. Before you back up anything, do a little disk housekeeping and delete all the unnecessary files that are cluttering it up. You'll be surprised at how many files you can get rid of, such as really old data files (you can put these on a floppy for long-term storage) and old README files that you've already read.*

*Then, once you've slimmed down your disk and put the files you work with regularly in one or two directories, use MSBACKUP and back up just those directories. Before you leave MSBACKUP, choose Save Setup As from the File menu. You'll be asked to give your setup a name and de-*

*scription so you can use these same selections again. For example, if you're backing up a couple of directories every week, you might want to name the setup file WEEKLY.SET (DOS adds the .SET extension for you). That way, you can just select the WEEKLY setup file when you do your weekly backup, and MSBACKUP will back up the directories you specified, without your having to remember which ones they were, which options you chose, or anything else about them. You can create as many as 50 different setup files that can cover just about any backup situation.*

# Undeleting What You Deleted by Mistake

When you install DOS 6, you can also install the Microsoft Undelete utility for DOS, for Windows, or for both. Even if you don't install it, you'll still have some chance of undeleting files you deleted by mistake, just by using the UNDELETE command.

If you installed Microsoft Undelete, you'll need to choose what kind of deletion protection you want—Delete Sentry or Delete Tracker. With Delete Sentry, you can be sure that you'll be able to get just about anything you delete back. Delete Sentry creates a hidden directory and stores everything you delete there (it empties this directory after it gets to be a certain size). So if what you delete isn't really deleted, you stand a pretty good chance of getting it back. With Delete Tracker, DOS just keeps track of where deleted files go, according to its own internal scheme of disk addresses. Deleted files aren't really deleted; the space they occupy is simply marked as available, and the next chance DOS gets, it will put a new file in that space. Once a new a file overwrites an old one like this, you or the Norton Utilities or anybody else won't be able to get the old one back. So Delete Tracker is less safe than Delete Sentry, but Delete Sentry requires a certain amount of disk real estate to work.

Although you can turn on either method of deletion protection just by typing *undelete /s* (for Delete Sentry) or *undelete /t* (for Tracker) at the command line, you'll probably forget to do it until *after* you've deleted a file by mistake. The safest thing to do is put one of these commands in your AUTOEXEC.BAT file. To use Delete Tracker, put this line in your AUTOEXEC.BAT: UNDELETE /S. For Delete Tracker, use the line UNDELETE /T. Chapter 10 tells you how to get into your AUTOEXEC.BAT file and change it.

No matter which scheme you choose, to undelete a file, simply type *undelete* and press Enter at the command prompt.

DOS 6 will figure out which kind of deletion protection you chose and do its best to retrieve the deleted file for you. If you're using Delete Sentry or Delete Tracker, it will ask you whether you want to undelete each file that has been deleted from the directory you're in. If you know the name of the file, save yourself some time and just type *undelete* followed by the file's name.

If you're not using one of the new protection schemes, you may still be able to recover a file with the "old" undelete method. If DOS reports that the MS-DOS directory contains any deleted files that can be recovered, type *undelete /dos* at the command prompt and press Enter. You'll be prompted for the first character in each file's name; just enter any character, and DOS will undelete the file.

See the Appendix for details on how to go back and install Microsoft Undelete if you didn't install it along with DOS 6. If you're not sure whether one or the other has been installed, try deleting a file and then undeleting it to find out. This is good practice anyway, because when the time comes to *really* undelete a file you deleted by mistake, you'll probably be in a panic (me, too).

# Protecting Against Viruses

How can you tell if you have a virus? Your computer may slow to a crawl, or you may see strange things on the screen, along with new and unusual error messages. Viruses are *no fun*; they usually mean that you're going to have to reformat your hard disk, which destroys everything that's on it. DOS 6 comes with a virus protection program called VSAFE that can constantly monitor your system for you, or you can check for viruses only when you want to by using the MSAV command.

The best protection is to put the line VSAFE in your AUTOEXEC.BAT file so that virus protection will be on all the time. See Chapter 10 for how to change your AUTOEXEC.BAT file.

To scan for viruses with MSAV (the "manual" virus protection program), type *msav* at the command prompt. You'll see this screen:

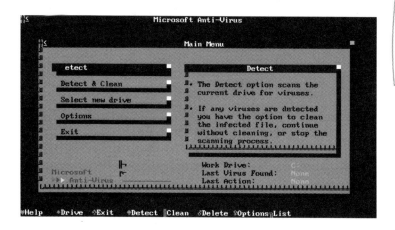

**TIP—** *You can put the line MSAV /P instead in your AUTOEXEC.BAT instead of VSAFE, and MSAV will run only when your computer starts up. VSAFE runs all the time, and it's better protection.*

To scan your hard drive (assuming you started MSAV from your hard drive), choose Detect & Clean. If you want to be prompted if a virus is found and asked what you want to do about it, choose Detect instead.

To scan a floppy drive, choose Select New Drive and pick the drive you want to scan.

If a virus is located, you'll see a screen showing you the actions you can take (try to repair the file, continue to scan, or stop). I hope you never see one!

**TIP—** *Be prepared to sit there for a while if you're scanning a big hard disk. MSAV will stop if certain options are on and it detects a file that's been changed since the last time you ran the virus-protection program, and you'll need to tell it what to do next. If you know the change is OK, choose Update so you won't be bothered the next time you scan your hard disk.*

**INSTALLING NEW PROGRAMS WITH VSAFE ON**

When you upgrade programs to a new version, the anti virus program senses the activity and assumes that a virus is causing it. To keep annoying "the-sky-is-falling" messages to a minimum, run MSAV on the installation disks first. Then write-protect them (open the hole on a 3.5-inch disk; cover the notch on a 5.25-inch disk). Then install the new program.

## Belt-and-Suspenders Protection

If you get a virus, you may not be able to use your hard disk. To protect yourself, make a floppy disk that has MSAV on it (so maybe it can repair your hard disk) and that you can use to start your computer.

**1.** Put a floppy disk in drive A.

**2.** Type *format a: /s.* This puts the DOS system files on it so you can use it to start your computer. If you ever need to use it, put the disk in drive A and turn on the power.

**3.** Type *copy msav*.* a:* to copy the MSAV files onto the floppy disk.

**4.** Take it out of the drive and label it "emergency anti-virus floppy." To make sure that this emergency disk doesn't get infected, too, write-protect it. (Open the hole of a 3.5-inch disk; cover the tab of a 5.25-inch disk.)

## Keep Your Virus Protection Current

People have to keep their vaccinations current, and so do computers. New viruses are appearing all the time. Central Point Software (the maker of the DOS 6 anti-virus programs) maintains a hot line where you can check for the latest vicious viruses and get your virus list updated. That number is 503/690-2660. If you have a modem, call 503/690-6650 for the electronic bulletin board, where you can download the latest files.

> **TIP—** *To see the list of viruses you're protected against, press F9 when you're looking at the MSAV screen.*

# Here's How To...

| | |
|---|---|
| **Copy an entire floppy disk** | Choose Disk Copy from the Disk Utilities group, or use the DOS DISKCOPY command |
| **Copy selected files or single directory** | Choose Copy from the File **a** menu, or use the DOS COPY command |
| **Copy files in a directory** | Use the DOS XCOPY command |
| **Undelete files you've deleted by mistake** | Type *undelete* at the command prompt |
| **Back up and restore files on a hard disk** | Type *msbackup* at the command prompt |
| **Run an anti-virus program** | Type *msav* at the command prompt |
| **Keep virus protection on all the time** | Put the line VSAFE in your AUTOEXEC.BAT file |

**Paper remembers so that you can forget.**

—Motto of the Nelson Printing Company
Spokane, Washington
Adolph Nelson, proprietor, circa 1933

# Printing

You'll probably print most of the time by using one of your programs like Microsoft Word or Borland's Quattro Pro (I'm trying to be democratic by mentioning all sorts of programs), but there are ways to print directly from DOS.

## Screen Dumps

You can get a copy of what's on your screen (called a **screen dump**) by pressing the Print Screen key. If you don't see a Print Screen key on your keyboard, look for one marked PrtSc. Press Shift and PrtSc at the same time to get a screen dump. Just make sure your printer's on and its "on line" light is lit before you do this, or your computer may hang up, and you'll have to restart it.

## Printing a File

You can use the Shell's Print command or the DOS PRINT command to print text-only files (unformatted files).

In the Shell, choose Command Prompt from the Main group

> **TIP—** *If you're going to print from the Shell, you have to first give the PRINT command at the command line, or Run it from the File menu.*

and give the PRINT command. Then return to the Shell and select the file or files you want to print. You can then choose Print from the File menu. The files will be added to the list of files that are being printed, called the **print queue.**

If you use the DOS PRINT command, you have more control over how a file is to be printed. You can specify which printer to use and see what's in the print queue, for example.

For example, to print a file named DEC.TXT by using the command line, enter the command as *print dec.txt.* You'll be asked for the name of the device you want to use; just press Enter to use your printer, if you've only got one.

## Checking the Queue

To see what's in the print queue, just use the PRINT command by itself at the DOS command line, like this: *print.* DOS will show you a list of all the files that are scheduled for printing.

### FIGURING OUT WHERE YOUR PRINTER'S ATTACHED

PRN means "the printer on the first parallel printer port," which is where most folks hook up their printer. If you have a printer connected to a serial port, like COM1, or if you have more than one printer, you'll need to tell DOS which port to use. There are two kinds of ports: **parallel ports** (called LPT1, LPT2, and so forth) and **serial ports** (called COM1, COM2,

etc.). Dot-matrix printers commonly use parallel ports, and laser printers often use serial ports, but not always. Here's how to tell which port your printer is on (of course you could always look at the back of your computer, but mine is a bunch of spaghetti back there, and yours probably is, too).

Turn your printer on. Then, at the DOS prompt, enter

    copy con lpt1 (press Enter)

    testing (press Enter)

Then press F6 and Enter. If it prints, your printer's on LPT1.

If not, try LPT2, LPT3, COM1, COM2, and COM3 in the first line until the pesky thing prints. (With some laser or inkjet printers you may need to push the form feed button to get them to print.)

Now you know which port your printer's on. If it's not on LPT1, give the PRINT command like this, specifying which port your printer's on with the /d option:

    print test.txt /d:com1
    (use the name of your file instead of TEST.TXT).

## Printing as You Type

If you want to print as you type at the keyboard, enter the command as *copy con prn* (CON is your console, or keyboard) and press Enter. Then type whatever you want the printer to print. When you've finished typing, press F6 and Enter. The printer will then start printing what you typed. (Try pressing the form feed button if it doesn't.)

# Here's How To...

| | |
|---|---|
| **Get a printout of the screen** | Press Shift-Print Screen |
| **Print a file or files** | Use the DOS PRINT command at the command line; then you can use the File menu's Print command |
| **Cancel all printing** | Use the PRINT /t command at the command line |
| **See what's in the print queue** | Use the PRINT command at the command line |
| **Print as you type** | Use the COPY command at the command line as *copy con prn* |

**Knowledge is of two kinds: we know a subject ourselves, or we know where we can find information about it.** —BOSWELL's *Life of Dr. Johnson*, 1791

# AUTOEXEC.BAT and CONFIG.SYS

DOS uses two special files called AUTOEXEC.BAT and CONFIG.SYS each time you start your computer. They tell it which commands to execute as it starts up and prepare it to use the "devices," like a mouse or an extra disk drive, that you might have. Most of the time you don't have to know much about these special files. But there may be times when you *will* need to know something about them—if you buy new programs that want to change your AUTOEXEC.BAT file or if you get new hardware. You can look them up here then. Don't worry about them unless you have to, because some of this can get kind of technical.

> **TIP—** *Most of what's in this chapter is stuff you'll probably never need to know. But it's here if you need it.*

## AUTOEXEC.BAT

As part of its normal routine each time you start your computer, DOS checks a special file called AUTOEXEC.BAT and executes the commands that it finds in it. These commands usually include, at a minimum, the path of directories and subdirectories leading to where DOS and the programs you use most frequently are stored. You can put commands in your

AUTOEXEC.BAT file that will do other things, such as make sure that everything you save is double-checked or set up a custom prompt for you instead of the standard C>.

To see what's in your AUTOEXEC.BAT file by using the Shell, just highlight it (it'll be in your root directory) and press F9. (Or use the DOS TYPE command to see it by entering *type autoexec.bat* at the command line.) You'll probably see something like this, but yours won't be exactly like this one:

> **TIP**— *The AUTOEXEC.BAT file executes whenever you start your computer, even if you restart it with Ctrl-Alt-Del.*

    @ECHO OFF

    PROMPT $P$G

    PATH C:\;C:\DOS;C:\WP51

    C:\DOS\DOSSHELL

These cryptic lines tell DOS not to display the AU-TOEXEC.BAT file as it executes (the @ECHO OFF turns off the display); to set your prompt to show the path to the current directory (the PROMPT $P$G line); to let you run DOS commands and start WordPerfect 5.1 from any directory, even if you're not in the DOS or WP51 directories; and to start the Shell running each time you start your computer.

> **TIP**— *Your AUTOEXEC-.BAT file may be a lot more complex (or a lot simpler) than this one. If your system is running fine and you don't need to change it, don't change it!*

# Changing Your AUTOEXEC.BAT File

You can add commands to your AUTOEXEC.BAT file by editing it with the Editor that comes with DOS or editing it with your favorite word processing program. (If you use a word processing program, be sure to save the revised AU-TOEXEC.BAT as a text-only file. See the Files chapter if you're not sure what this is.)

## Using the Editor

To use the DOS Editor for changing your AUTOEXEC.BAT file, highlight it and then choose Editor from the Main group. You'll be prompted for the name of the file to edit. Enter *autoexec.bat* and press Enter.

In the Editor, you can use the arrow keys or mouse to move around, use the Backspace and Del keys to delete what's there, or use the Edit menu to cut, copy, or paste lines. Just remember that in the AUTOEXEC.BAT file, each command must begin on a new, separate line.

**TIP—** *Keep the line with the DOSSHELL command in it as the last line in your AUTOEXEC.BAT file so that all the other things you want to do, like loading your mouse, will be done first, before the Shell comes up.*

```
  File   Edit   Search   Options                              Help
┌───────────────────────── AUTOEXEC.BAT ─────────────────────────┐
│ LH /L:1,37040 C:\PCACHE\PCACHE                                  ↑│
│ c:\win2\AD_WRAP.COM                                             │
│ SET BLASTER=A220 I7 D1 T3                                       │
│ LH /L:0:1,42384 /S C:\DOS\SMARTDRV.EXE                          │
│ @ECHO OFF                                                       │
│ PROMPT $p$g                                                     │
│ PATH C:\DOS;C:\GMKW;C:\INSTBASE;C:\WIN2;C:\WPC;C:\WPWIN;C:\;C:\NU;C:\TOPS;C:\W│
│ SET GMKW5=C:\GMKW                                               │
│ SET NU=C:\NU                                                    │
│ IMAGE                                                           │
│ SET TEMP=C:\DOS                                                 │
│ LH /L:1,65792 C:\DOS\COMMAND /E:256 /CC:\DOS\mouse              │
│ numoff                                                          │
│ ad-dos.com                                                      │
│ cls                                                             │
│ SET WSWWORK=C:\TEMP                                             │
│ SET SOUND=C:\SB                                                 │
│ LH /L:1,13984 C:\DOS\SHARE                                      │
│ rem win                                                         │
│ C:\DOS\SHARE.EXE   ▌                                            │
│ C:\DOS\MOUSE                                                   ↓│
├────────────────────────────────────────────────────────────────┤
│ MS-DOS Editor  <F1=Help> Press ALT to activate menus      00001:001│
└────────────────────────────────────────────────────────────────┘
```

*OK, I know I have a complex AUTOEXEC.BAT file. Yours will be simpler—and shorter, too.*

To add a new line, just type it and press Enter. When you're done, you can just choose Save from the File menu to save the file as AUTOEXEC.BAT (the Editor always saves files as text-only files, so you don't have to worry about using a special procedure), or use the Save As command to save it under a different name. You'll see a tip for why you might like to do this later in the chapter.

Now let's look at some of the ways you might want to change your AUTOEXEC.BAT file.

## Creating a Custom Prompt

DOS's Setup program alters your plain-vanilla DOS prompt (C>) to show the current path to whatever directory you're in by adding the line

PROMPT $p$g

to your AUTOEXEC.BAT file. So if you're in a subdirectory called SPREADS under an EXCEL directory on drive C, your prompt looks like this:

C:\EXCEL\SPREADS>

There are quite a few other things you can do to customize your DOS prompt, such as putting your name or the current date in it. Here's how you'd do your name:

PROMPT Your Name$g

The $g represents the > symbol. I'd get a prompt like *Kay Nelson>* (here DOS will tell the difference between upper- and lowercase). Just enter PROMPT to get the standard C> back.

See the PROMPT command in the DOS Commands section for some more examples; most of them require you to use some pretty cryptic symbols.

> **TIP**— *You might want to print out a copy of your AUTOEXEC.BAT file before you change it so that you can see what you did if things go wrong and your computer doesn't start the way you intended.*

## Setting up Delete Protection

You can set up DOS 6 so that files you undelete aren't really deleted. They're sent to an invisible directory that's emptied after it gets to be a certain size.

When you install DOS 6, you'll be asked whether you want to install the deletion protection utility for DOS, Windows, or both. That's the first step. The second step is to edit your AUTOEXEC.BAT file so that the protection will always be in effect. You'll be able to recover just about any file you delete by mistake—maybe not one you deleted last year, though. To do this, put an UNDELETE /S line in your AUTOEXEC.BAT for Delete Sentry (the safest method) or an UNDELETE /T line there for Delete Tracker. Chapter 8 discusses the differences between the two methods.

If you decide not to install deletion protection during setup, you can go back and add it later (see the Appendix). There are all sorts of switches you can use with them. You can get help on Undelete (**help undelete**) to see them all.

## Canceling AUTOEXEC.BAT Commands

Instead of deleting a command from your AUTOEXEC.BAT file, you can just stop it from being used by starting the line it's on with a REM command (for "remark"). For example, you may have a line in your AUTOEXEC.BAT file that starts some memory-resident program running. Many of these programs take up a lot of memory. If you think that a memory-resident program might be making your computer run slower or be causing other problems, you can temporarily stop it from running by starting its command line in the AUTOEXEC.BAT file with REM. To reactivate the command later, all you have to do is delete the REM, save the file, and restart your computer. Since you can see the lines you've disabled, you don't have to remember what you did if you want to enable them again later.

**TIP**—*If you always want to start with a program, put the command used to start it as the last line in the AUTOEXEC.BAT file. Otherwise it will start before AUTOEXEC.BAT finishes running. If you always want to start in the Shell, put the DOSSHELL line last.*

## Batch Files

Your AUTOEXEC.BAT file is a special kind of file called a **batch file.** A batch file is just a text file that ends in .BAT and consists of DOS commands, one per line. Writing a batch file lets you give DOS a set of instructions: "first, do this; then do that."

**TIP**— *You can test your changed AUTOEXEC-.BAT file without re-starting your computer by typing* autoexec *at the DOS prompt*

You can create other batch files with the built-in Editor, because it's designed to handle text-only files, and when you save a file with it, the file will automatically be a text file. DOS wants text, just text, and no formatting commands like those that word processing programs automatically put in.

**TIP**— *Most word processing programs will let you create text-only files, but it won't be in the "normal" way that you create documents with the program.*

Unfortunately, we don't have room here to go into too much detail about batch files. However, if you're interested in creating one that protects your AUTOEXEC.BAT from being altered, read the sidebar "Warning! Your AUTOEXEC.BAT Can Get Changed."

### WARNING! YOUR AUTOEXEC.BAT CAN GET CHANGED

*(fyi)*

Most programs that you buy come with their own installation programs that will automatically go into your AUTOEXEC.BAT file and change it to suit the way they run (some of them will ask you politely if it's all right to do this). They usually want to add themselves to your PATH command so that you can execute them from any directory, or do some other technical things. If all they want to do is get in your PATH, there's a way to keep them out (see the end of this section). Usually they'll rename your existing AUTOEXEC.BAT file as AUTOEXEC.OLD or AUTOEXEC.BAK, so you can go back and look at what's in the two files to see what the differences are. Normally what these programs do to your AUTOEXEC.BAT file is perfectly okay and even necessary if they're going to run properly, so leave the changes they make alone unless you're having trouble, like getting error messages about programs not running right.

However, if you find that installation programs are changing your AUTOEXEC.BAT file in ways that you don't want them to, there's a way you can prevent them from doing that. First, get your AUTOEXEC.BAT just as you want it; then save it as STARTUP.BAT (use the Editor to make sure that no invisible formatting commands get into it). Then create another AUTOEXEC.BAT file that consists of just these two lines:

    @ECHO OFF

    CALL STARTUP.BAT

# CONFIG.SYS

DOS also executes another file called CONFIG.SYS when it starts up. This is your system configuration file . It tells DOS what kinds of devices—like external disk drives or a mouse— are connected to your computer, how many files can be used at a time, and so forth. Normally, you'll never need to change this file. However, some auto-installation programs will go in and change it for you to suit the way they run, so it's a good idea to know that CONFIG.SYS is there and a little bit about it so that you can respond intelligently to those "Change CONFIG.SYS?" prompts.

> **TIP—** *If you ever need to change a line in your CONFIG.SYS file, be sure to save it as a text file (use the Editor to make sure). Restart your computer for the change to take effect.*

## Buffers

One of the most common things installation programs do is change the number of files and buffers allowed. A **buffer** is a

And save it as AUTOEXEC.BAT!

From now on, you can let installation programs alter your AUTOEXEC.BAT file as much as they want to. When the installation program is done, you can take a look at your AUTOEXEC.BAT file (the differences will be obvious, since it started out as just two simple lines) and either edit your STARTUP.BAT file to include the changes, or delete them.

As for letting a bunch of programs put themselves in your PATH statement, you don't have to. Instead, create a simple batch file for each program that changes to its directory and starts the program. For example, say that WordPerfect is stored in a WP51 directory on drive C, and the command used to start WordPerfect is WP (which it is). Create a batch file that changes to the WP51 directory and starts WordPerfect, like this:

　　COPY CON WP.BAT
　　{press Enter}

　　CD C:\WP51 {Enter}

　　WP {Enter}

^Z {press F6} {press Enter}

Now store that batch file in a directory where you keep all your batch files, say C:\BATCH. Do this for any program that you want to keep out of your path (a long path can slow you down, and a path can only be 127 characters long). Keep C:\BATCH in your path instead of all those paths to programs! And remember that Windows keeps track of where its programs are anyway, so don't let those installation programs buffalo you into garbaging up your path.

```
 File  Edit  Search  Options                              Help
                          CONFIG.SYS
DEVICE=C:\DOS\SETVER.EXE
DEVICE=C:\DOS\HIMEM.SYS
DEVICE=C:\DOS\EMM386.EXE NOEMS d=64 X=C400-C7FF
BUFFERS=24,0
FILES=30
DOS=UMB
LASTDRIVE=E
FCBS=16,0
DOS=HIGH
SHELL=C:\DOS\COMMAND.COM C:\DOS\ /p




                         I



+                                                    →
MS-DOS Editor  <F1=Help> Press ALT to activate menus      00001:001
```

part of memory (random-access memory, not disk storage space) that DOS uses to hold the information that it reads from disk. It's faster to read from RAM than from a disk, so having buffers lets DOS hold in RAM the information that's most likely to be needed next and access it quickly.

How many buffers should you have? If you've got a full 640K of RAM, probably 20 or 30. If you have a hard disk that's bigger than 80 Mb, you can use 40 or 50 buffers with no problem. It's best just to let the auto-installation programs set the number of buffers for you unless you look at your CONFIG.SYS file and see that you've only got 8, or some small number like that (unless you're using a disk cache, which does the same thing that BUFFERS does).

## Files

FILES is another setting you'll see in your CONFIG.SYS file, and it's also one that you may be prompted about when those auto-installation programs run. The FILES statement tells DOS the maximum number of files to keep track of at one time. Some programs need to have a lot of files open at one time—dBASE III+ likes to have 20, for example. If you start getting error messages about having too many files open, increase the FILES= number in your CONFIG.SYS file.

## Devices

You'll probably see a few other commands in your CON-
FIG.SYS file, too. DEVICE= is a command that tells DOS
what kind of hardware you're using. Normally, when you get
a new piece of equipment, like a mouse or a disk drive, its installation program will put a DEVICE= statement in your
CONFIG.SYS file so that DOS will know it's there. You'll
usually never need to change these things.

> **TIP**— *What comes after the = is called a device driver program. It usually ends in .SYS, too. Now you know.*

## Optimizing Memory

Your computer, without doubt, has 640K of **conventional
memory.** But it may have more memory than that. It gets
complicated. Before DOS 6, you had to know all sorts of
things about memory so that you could make intelligent de-
cisions about what to put in your CONFIG.SYS file. However, DOS 6 comes with a marvelous utility called MEM-
MAKER that analyzers your system and optimizes memory
usage for you. If you're not interested in what memory does or
where it is or anything like that, just run MEMMAKER and
let it take care of everything for you.

> **TIP**— *Tip: If you don't have a 386 (or higher) computer, you can't use MEMMAKER, so skip to the boring part called The Hard Stuff about Memory.*

## Using MEMMAKER

To run MEMMAKER, you'll need a 386 or higher computer.
To start, you should be at the DOS prompt. Type **memmaker** and press Enter. Follow the instructions on the screen.

Choose Express optimization, the default choice. A Custom
optimization option lets you specify what you want to put in
upper memory, if you're sure about what it is and a host of
other things. If you're curious about how MEMMAKER
works and what it does, press F1 when you're at the options
screen, after you've started MEMMAKER.

> **WARNING**— *don't exit to DOS temporarily from the Shell or from Windows before you run MEMMAKER. Exit completely.*

## The Hard Stuff about Memory

If you don't have a 386 computer, you can't use MEM-MAKER, so here are all the boring details you may need to know about memory.

If your system has extended memory, DOS can use part of it. Normally, the Setup program will be able to tell whether you have extended memory and will set DOS up to use it. You can check to see that your CONFIG.SYS file has the lines

> TIP— *DOS 6 comes with lots of Help screens for memory commands. At the command line, type* help emm386, help devicehigh, help load-high, help himem.sys, *or* help *followed by whatever command you need help on!*

DEVICE = HIMEM.SYS

DOS = HIGH

If CONFIG.SYS doesn't have these lines and the MEM command tells you that you have extended memory, add these lines to your CONFIG.SYS file and save it (use the Editor). This will make more memory available to your programs.

## More about Memory

There are several different kinds of memory. You can skip this memory lane part if you don't care, or come back to it later when you want to know the difference between extended memory and expanded memory. (I always mix them up.) And you may never have to know.

> TIP— *Use the MEM command to see what kind of memory you have.*

Back when IBM designed their PC, they decided that 640K of random-access memory (RAM) was the most anybody would ever need. But in their own typical IBM fashion, they left a whole megabyte of space for this 640K of conventional memory. Programs that run with DOS normally use conventional memory, and a lot of programs can't use any other kind.

The computer designers reserved the space between 640K and 1 Mb, which is 384K, because as you may or may not recall, 1 Mb is 1024K, the way computer people count. In this 384K of **reserved memory,** they figured everybody would put video adapter memory for the displays you see on your screen. Well, it didn't work out that way: everybody needed more RAM but not that much video memory. But the hardware was set up so that programs couldn't store information in that area, and so it just sat there, unused, until DOS 5 came along. We'll get back to this fascinating bit of history in a minute.

In the meantime, folks were scrabbling to figure out how to get around the carefully designed built-in limitations of the hardware and add more memory to DOS-type personal computers. (Hey, the Macintosh started out with a big 128K of RAM, but the Apple people didn't box themselves in like the IBM/Microsoft folks did!) So they came up with **memory manager programs** to get around it. To use this new-style memory, called **expanded memory** and **extended memory,** you have to also use one of these memory manager programs (one comes with your extra memory when you buy it). DOS also comes with two more memory managers for extended memory, maybe more, depending on how you're counting. You've seen how that counting stuff goes.

## EXPANDED MEMORY

There are two kinds of extra memory that you can add. Expanded memory can be added to most computers. Extended memory—the other kind—can be added only to 286 and higher computers.

The way expanded memory works is a little tricky: memory in an added memory board just gets swapped in and out by a memory manager, like the con artist and the shell game. You can think of it as being there, but not in any given place. A lot of folks think that expanded memory is that 384K space above conventional memory, but it's not. You can have more than 384K of expanded memory, and your memory manager just swaps it around for you. DOS doesn't have any special manager for expanded memory; you just use the one that came with the added board. Some programs can use expanded memory; others can't.

## CHAPTER 10

## EXTENDED MEMORY

Most 286 and higher computers come with more memory than one megabyte, and that's called **extended memory.** It's above the 640K of conventional memory and the mysterious 384K that's sometimes called the upper memory block, reserved memory, or even (incorrectly) high memory. DOS has special managers for your extended memory.

> **TIP**— *Extended memory is the kind that Windows loves to use. You have to have a 286 or higher computer to use it.*

Now the difference between extended memory and expanded memory is in how DOS and your programs use it. Instead of fooling programs about what memory they're really using like expanded memory does, extended memory actually changes the way the processor accesses memory. Think of it as extending its arm out to grab more memory all over the place. (That's oversimplified, of course, but why did they have to make it so *hard?*) Most of DOS (after version 5) can go in and run in extended memory, leaving more of the other, conventional kind of memory available to your programs. And that's good.

Setup will automatically set you up to use extended memory, as we said earlier, with the extended memory manager that comes with DOS 5 and 6, called HIMEM.SYS. And it will load most of DOS into the **high memory area (HMA),** which is the first 64K beyond the 1 Mb line.

## GOT A 386? READ ON.

Now it gets more complex. If I were you at this point I would close this book and get out the manual to get the gory details. Better yet, I would have run MEMMAKER and never have reached this part of the book at all. But just to give you an overview, read on.

If you have a 386 or 486 computer, you can use a memory manager called EMM386 that comes with DOS. Setup doesn't automatically do anything with this one; you have to put it into your CONFIG.SYS file yourself with a line like

    DEVICE = C:\DOS\EMM386.EXE NOEMS

Or, of course, you can run MEMMAKER and have it take care of that.

EMM386 allows some of the extended memory to be used as expanded memory, for programs that can use expanded but not extended memory. But the NOEMS in the example line says "don't use expanded memory." If your programs can use it, you'll want to use the RAM switch instead of NOEMS and specify how much expanded memory to use, like 640 RAM to use 640K of expanded memory.

You can also use EMM386 to manage that unused memory in the upper memory block, the one that was designed in and then left alone. Once you've set DOS up to use it, you can load programs into it by using the LOADHIGH command (there are some examples of it in the DOS Commands section). The trick is that you've got to be using HIMEM and EMM386, both, for DOS to use the upper memory block. So if you've done all the stuff above and you've got HIMEM and EMM386 in your CONFIG.SYS file, add UMB to the end of the DOS = HIGH line, like this:

    DOS = HIGH, UMB

Now that you've done all that, you can load programs into your high memory area, because DOS has been prepared to use it. Just get out the manual.

## Logical Drives

What else might you see in a CONFIG.SYS file? LAST-DRIVE tells DOS how many disk drives you have. Normally drives A and B are your floppy disk drives and C and D are hard disk drives. DOS throws in another one, just for fun: drive E, even if you don't have five disk drives. These don't

TIP— *Logical drives are also sometimes called virtual drives.*

have to be real, physical disk drives that you can touch: they can be "logical" drives. A logical drive is—well, it's one that doesn't physically exist but it acts as if it does (this is logical?). A RAM disk is an example of a logical drive. Network drives are also logical drives. If you add more hard disk drives to your system, you may need to increase the letter of the LAST-DRIVE.

## Other CONFIG.SYS Commands

You may see other commands in your CONFIG.SYS file. These are special DOS commands that can't be entered on the command line (except for BREAK) but that tell DOS special things about your system.

One last thing that you may see in your CONFIG.SYS file is an INSTALL= statement. This is used to load four special memory-resident commands: FASTOPEN, SHARE, KEYB, and NLSFUNC. Those last two are for when you're switching from one international setting to another. FASTOPEN tells DOS how many files to keep track of, so it can speed up your system's performance, and SHARE is used when you're on a network.

# Here's How To...

| | |
|---|---|
| **See what's in your AUTOEXEC.BAT or CONFIG.SYS file** | Highlight it and press F9, or TYPE AUTOEXEC.BAT (or CONFIG.SYS) at the command prompt |
| **Use the Editor** | Choose Editor from the Main group in the Shell, or enter *edit* at the command prompt |
| **Cancel a command in your AUTOEXEC.BAT file** | Start the line it's on with REM |
| **Create a batch file** | Use the Editor and put one DOS command per line. Give the file a .BAT extension when you name it. |
| **Cancel a command in your CONFIG.SYS file** | Press F8 when you see the "Starting MS-DOS..." message; type **Y** or **N** for each line in the CONFIG.SYS |
| **Bypass your AUTOEXEC.BAT and CONFIG.SYS files** | Press F5 when you see the "Starting MS-DOS..." message |

**"I had it right, but I got it wrong."**
—Late twentieth-century Country/Western song,
author unknown

# DOS Commands

DOS is very picky about how it wants you to enter commands. If you misspell a command, you'll get a "Bad command or file name" message. This doesn't mean that the command was bad, just that you probably typed it wrong. And DOS isn't always logical. For example, you can abbreviate the DELETE command as DEL, but you can't shorten the ERASE command (which does the same thing as DEL) to ERA.

This section will show you how to enter all the DOS commands just the way DOS wants them. It will also show you a lot of examples of how to use the options—those cryptic letters that are preceded by a slash that tell DOS how you want the command carried out.

Recall from Chapter 3 that a command consists of three parts: the command itself, followed (sometimes) by what you want it to act on (the parameters), followed (sometimes) by an option or two.

DOS doesn't care whether you use uppercase or lowercase, and for the most part, it doesn't care a lot about spacing. Just remember always to leave a space between the command itself and what follows it. But DIR /W /P is just the same as DIR /W/P (which is, of course, the same as *dir /w /p)*. Don't worry about the spacing between options or whether letters are

> **Tip**— *There are other commands, like those for batch files, but this is a "little" DOS book.*

capitalized. I've capitalized the DOS commands themselves to distinguish them from the Shell commands that you can pick from menus.

Sometimes you'll need to use a colon (:) with an option. Just look carefully at the examples. If you leave the colon out, you can get one of those rebuking messages.

**TIP—** *You can get help at the command line by typing help and the name of the command you want help on and pressing Enter.*

If you've used DOS before, this section will help remind you of what to do so that you don't have to remember the picky little details. But a few commands you may be used to in DOS 5 are gone from DOS 6. Among them:

| | |
|---|---|
| **ASSIGN** | Use SUBST instead |
| **BACKUP** | Use MSBACKUP |
| **COMP** | Use FC |
| **GRAFTABL** | Never understood it anyway |
| **MIRROR** | Use new switches with UNDELETE instead |
| **RECOVER** | Never worked anyway |

If you need any of these commands (so that an old favorite batch file will work, for example), you can get them on a Supplemental Disk you can order from Microsoft (see the back of your manual). Just send the coupon you'll find there in to get a printed Help manual and the Supplemental Disk with the DOS commands that were in DOS 5 but not in DOS 6. The AccessDOS program is also on the Supplemental Disk; it makes DOS easier to use by people who are physically challenged. For example, it has utilities that change the keyboard layout to one that's easier to use if you type with only your right or left hand.

A few commands are new in DOS 6:

| | |
|---|---|
| **DEFRAG** | Optimizes your hard disk |
| **DELTREE** | Lets you delete directories |
| **FASTHELP** | Displays a list of DOS commands and what they do |
| **INTERLNK, INTERSVR** | Let you connect two computers and share files |
| **LOADFIX** | Ensures that a program loads into a certain area of memory |
| **MEMMAKER** | Optimizes your system's memory |
| **MOVE** | Lets you move files and directories without copying and deleting them |
| **MSAV** | Scans your computer for viruses |
| **MSBACKUP** | Replaces the BACKUP command |
| **MSD** | Displays information about your system |
| **MSCDEX** | Loads a CD-ROM driver |
| **NUMLOCK** | Finally! Turns Num Lock off on startup |
| **POWER** | Manages power on a portable computer |
| **SMARTDRV** | Creates a disk cache (technically "new;" in DOS 5, this wasn't a command but a device driver) |
| **VSAFE** | Monitors your computer for viruses |

Don't panic! There are only a few commands you'll use every day. They're the ones that have to do with seeing what's on your disks; copying, renaming, and deleting files; copying, formatting, and checking disks; getting help when you need it; checking the date and time; and clearing the screen.

Most of the DOS commands are obscure ones, or the ones you'll use once or twice only. They're all listed alphabetically so you can look up one or two of them if you ever need to use them.

Remember, you can get more help on any of DOS 6's commands just by typing **help** plus the name of the command at the command prompt and then pressing Enter.

# APPEND

Use APPEND to specify the directories that contain files a program needs. It lets you run programs without having to change to the directories that contain them.

## How to Enter It

APPEND directories to be searched

## Examples

APPEND C:\LETTERS lets you use all the files in the \LETTERS directory just as if they were really in your current directory.

APPEND A:\MEMOS;B:\DOCS lets you use the files in a directory called MEMOS on drive A and a directory called DOCS on drive B as though they were in the current directory. Notice that the paths are separated by semicolons.

APPEND shows you all the directories that are currently appended.

APPEND ; removes the list of appended directories so that DOS searches only the current directory for files.

## Details

APPEND is one of those commands that is used most often with older programs that don't let you put your program files in one directory and other files that the program needs in another. WordStar Release 3 is one of these.

If you regularly use programs that need the APPEND command to find files in other directories, you can put it in your AUTOEXEC.BAT file along with the directories so that you don't have to type it again (APPEND C:\LETTERS, for example). See Chapter 10.

How is APPEND different from PATH? The PATH command lets you specify directories to be searched for executable files (programs); APPEND lets you specify data files. You should use PATH in your AUTOEXEC.BAT file, for sure.

There are some exotic options you can use with APPEND, but we won't go into detail about them here because you use them mostly if you're working with programming tools.

# ATTRIB

Use ATTRIB to make a file read-only (protect it from being changed) or, during a backup or copy procedure, to mark which files have been backed up or copied.

## How to Enter It

ATTRIB *options* **filename**

**TIP**— *In the Shell, choose Change Attributes from the file menu.*

## Examples

**ATTRIB +r REPORT.DOC** protects the file REPORT.DOC from being changed or erased, although you can read it. (The options +r and -r turn a file's read-only attribute on and off.)

**ATTRIB -r A:\REPORTS\OCT /S** removes the read-only protection from the files in the REPORTS\OCT directory on drive A as well as from the files in any subdirectories under it. (The /S option specifies that all the files in any subdirectories are to be affected by ATTRIB.)

**ATTRIB +a \*.\*** turns on the archive attribute for all the files in the current directory (you'd add the /S option if you wanted to turn it on for all the files in any subdirectories, too). This makes sure that they will all be included in the next backup, whether they've been modified or not. (The options +a and -a turn a file's archive attribute on and off.)

**ATTRIB EXAMPLE.DOC** reports whether the read-only and the archive attributes are on or off for the file.

**TIP**— *You can use wildcards with ATTRIB.*

## Details

The options +s and -s let you set a file as a system file, but you probably don't want to do this anyway.

DOS normally turns on the archive attribute when you create or change a file. When you do a backup or copy a bunch of files with XCOPY, you may sometimes want to turn on the archive attribute for a file that hasn't been changed, so that it will be backed up or copied, too. You can also turn off the archive attribute for a file that has been changed if you don't want to include it in the backup or copy procedure. See MSBACKUP and XCOPY also.

# BREAK

Use BREAK to specify that you can press Ctrl-Break or Ctrl-C to stop a program any time it's running, not just during keyboard and screen operations, which is the normal setting.

## How to Enter It

**BREAK ON, BREAK OFF**

turns BREAK on and off;

**BREAK**

shows whether Break is on or not.

## Details

Normally DOS interrupts, or breaks, when you press Ctrl-C only if an operation that uses the keyboard, screen, or printer is under way. If you turn on BREAK, processes like saving a file will be interrupted when you press Ctrl-C.

Most programs have a special way for you to stop them gracefully, without destroying any data that may be being saved. It's best to leave BREAK alone in most cases. The only logical reason I've ever heard of for using it is if you're testing programs of unknown origin and want an instant way to bail out if something starts going wrong.

# CD

Use CD to change to a different directory.

## How to Enter It

**CD path**

## Examples

**CD \LOTUS** changes your current directory to LOTUS.

**CD** displays the name of the current directory.

**CD ..** moves you up one level in the directory structure.

**CD \** takes you directly to the root directory.

> **TIP**— *Just highlight a directory in the Shell to change to it.*

## Details

If you want to change to a directory that's a subdirectory of the directory you're in, you don't need to type the backslash. For example, if you're in a directory named WINTER that has a subdirectory named DEC, you can type CD DEC.

> **TIP**— *Remember the shortcuts .. and \ (see the examples). They can save you time.*

One of the commonest mistakes you can make is to create a directory (with MD, for Make Directory) and then forget to change to it with CD.

The CD command doesn't change the current drive. To change the current drive, type A: or B: or C: at the DOS prompt (remember the colon).

You can also use CHDIR instead of CD, but why bother?

# CHCP

Use CHCP to change the code page (character set) your computer uses, or to display the code number for the character set that's in effect.

## How to Enter It

CHCP code page number

## Examples

**CHCP 863** sets the current character set to French-Canadian.

## Details

It's not as easy as you think! CHCP is only one of several commands you use if you want to use DOS's international language support features. You first have to use the NLSFUNC command to tell DOS where a file named COUNTRY.SYS is (this file has the information about the date and time formats and special symbols for different countries). You then have to use the MODE command to prepare the code pages you want to be able to use and then select which one is to be active. You then have to load a new keyboard translation table with the KEYB command. (You still there?) *Then* you can use CHCP to switch between code pages. Better get somebody else to do it, or get out one of those thousand-page books and settle down for the evening.

TIP— *You don't need to do any of this unless you're trying to use a PC bought in the United States for work in a language other than English.*

Code 437 is U.S., 850 is Multinational, 860 is Portuguese, 863 is French-Canadian, and 865 is Nordic.

# CHKDSK

Use CHKDSK to check your disk to see how much free space is left on it, see how much RAM is available, and fix errors on the disk.

## How to Enter It

**CHKDSK drive:** *options*

## Examples

**CHKDSK** checks the current disk and reports its volume name, date of creation, storage capacity, number of files, amount of free space, number of bad sectors, and so forth.

**CHKDSK A:** checks the disk in drive A.

**CHKDSK /F** checks the disk and also "fixes" errors that it finds on the disk, like fragmented files, lost clusters, and bad sectors (these terms all refer to the way DOS physically stores data on the disk).

**CHKDSK /V** displays the name of each file as it's being checked.

## Details

Using CHKDSK with the /F option locates bits of files that have been separated from the files they belong to (these are called "lost clusters"). If CHKDSK finds any of these, it asks you whether you want them converted to files. If you say Yes, it will convert those unusable bits of files to numbered files that end in .CHK, and you can then delete them all (DEL *.CHK) to get rid of them and free up more space on the disk. You can also look at them and see what they contain and try to figure

> **TIP**— *Get out one of those thousand-page tomes if you want to find out about all the various kinds of problems that can happen to a disk.*

out which file they belong to, but it's usually a waste of time, since they're probably unusable anyway.

If you get the message "Convert directory to file?" it basically means that everything in the directory is garbage. (Converting it to a file may help you learn what *was* there, though.)

If you give the command as CHKDSK *.*, CHKDSK will check to see whether files are contiguous (stored next to each other) or not. If they aren't, your disk operations are slower than they could be. Use DOS 6's new DEFRAG command to optimize your hard disk by gathering up and storing related bits of files next to each other instead of keeping them scattered all over the disk.

You can also speed up disk operations by using COPY (or XCOPY) to copy the files on the disk onto a different disk. (When files are copied, they are put back next to each other again, in the right order.) Don't use DISKCOPY, though, or you'll just transfer the problem from one disk to another!

Don't panic if CHKDSK reports bad sectors. These are unreliable parts of the disk that were ignored when it was formatted.

# CLS

Use CLS to clear the screen and reposition the cursor in the upper-left corner.

## How to Enter It

CLS

CLS just clears the screen; it doesn't affect anything that you've saved.

You can also use CLS in batch files, if you need to present information on a new, blank screen, for example.

# COMMAND

Use COMMAND to start another copy of DOS running.

## How to Enter It

COMMAND PATH *options*

Sometimes you may want to start another copy of DOS running. For example, if you're doing programming in Pascal or BASIC or some other language, you may want to execute a couple of DOS commands while you're in your program, and you can do that with the COMMAND command. If it's likely that you're going to do this, though, you're probably not reading this book. I'll just mention that when you give the command, you'll need to supply the path to where the command processor (the copy of DOS) is, and that the options will let you specify a new environment size and all sorts of other technical goodies. A /K switch, new in DOS 6, lets you execute a program or batch file before taking you to the DOS prompt.

# COPY

Use COPY to copy files. You can also use it to join files together.

## How to Enter It

COPY source file *options* destination *options*

## Examples

**COPY OCT.RPT OCT.BAK** makes a duplicate of the file OCT.RPT with a .BAK extension, so that you'll know it's a backup copy. The copy is made in the current directory.

> **TIP**— *In the Shell, choose Copy from the File menu or press F8.*

**COPY C:\SPREADS\OCT.RPT A:** copies the OCT.RPT file, which is not in the current directory, to a disk in drive A, naming the copy OCT.RPT, its original name.

**COPY A:*.* C: /V** copies all the files in the current directory of the disk in drive A to the current directory on your hard disk (drive C). It also verifies that each copy was made correctly, with the /V option.

**COPY CH? C:\LOTUS\REPORTS** copies all files in the current directory starting with CH and ending in one character, such as CH1, CH2, CH3, and so forth, to the LOTUS\REPORTS directory on drive C.

**COPY CON: DOIT.BAT** creates a batch file named DOIT consisting of whatever you type next after pressing Enter. The CON: means "console," or keyboard, so what you're doing is copying from the keyboard. Press F6 when you're through typing; this tells DOS that it's the end of the file.

> **TIP**— *This is the way to create simple batch files quickly.*

**COPY OCT.RPT+NOV.RPT DEC.RPT** combines the two files into a file named DEC.RPT. You can combine any number of files, not just two.

## Details

There are two exotic options, /A and /B. The first treats the file as if it were a text-only file, and the second treats it as a program (binary) file. You won't normally have to use the /A and /B options, but you may want to use /V to have DOS verify that each copy was made accurately.

Use COPY if you're copying only a few files, or files that have similar names, so that you can use the wildcards ? (for one character) and * (for any number of characters).

Use XCOPY if you're copying a large number of files, or if you want to copy files by date, or if you're copying entire directories and subdirectories.

Use DISKCOPY to duplicate disks.

Use MSBACKUP to back up large numbers of files on your hard disk to floppy disks in one of your floppy drives and restore them.

Use REN to rename files.

Before you erase your original files, make sure that the copies are really where you thought you copied them by changing to that directory and getting a listing of what's in it with the DIR command.

**TIP**— *Other commands that let you use wildcards: ATTRIB, BACKUP, CHKDSK, , DEL, DIR, ERASE, FC, PRINT, RECOVER, REN, REPLACE, RESTORE, UNDELETE, and XCOPY.*

**TIP**— *If DOS won't let you copy to a floppy disk and you get a "write-protect error" message, remove the write-protect tab from the disk (it's over the notch on the side). For a 3.5-inch disk, slide the plastic tab over the hole (close it).*

# CTTY

Use CTTY to change your standard input device, which is usually the keyboard. You could connect another terminal to your computer, for example.

## How to Enter It

**CTTY device**

## Examples

**CTTY COM3:** tells DOS to use a device connected to your COM3 port for input.

**CTTY CON:** returns control to your keyboard.

## Details

This is another command you probably won't use very often. One case where you might use it is to allow a machine connected via modem (on one of your COM ports) to provide input to your computer.

Note how you have to use the colon in both of the examples.

TIP— *The CTTY CON: command has to be issued from the remote terminal, which is currently in control.*

# DATE

Use DATE to display the system date, or set it.

## How to Enter It

**DATE**

tells you the system date;

**DATE MM-DD-YY**

lets you set the date (type the current date, not "mm-dd-yy").

## Details

You can enter DATE and then respond to the prompt by typing in a new date. If the date is OK, just press Enter.

When you type the date, you don't have to use leading zeroes to take up two spaces. For example, 2-6-93 is just as OK as 02-06-93. (If you type 00 as the year, DOS will assume it is the year 2000.) You can enter the year as 93 or 1993.

You can also use slashes or periods in the date: 2-6-93, 2/6/93, and 2.6.93 are all OK.

DOS keeps track of leap years and such, so you shouldn't have to set the date unless your system's clock batteries get low.

# DBLSPACE

Use DBLSPACE to compress your hard and floppy disks so they can store more data.

## How to Enter It

DBLSPACE

## Details

The DBLSPACE command, new with DOS 6, provides a menu interface that you can use to gain much more space on your disks. For details on it and examples, see Chapter 6.

# DEFRAG

Use DEFRAG to optimize your hard disk, usually, just after you install DOS 6.

## How to Enter It

```
DEFRAG
```

## Details

DOS 6 comes with a new DEFRAG command that will optimize your hard disk so that it runs faster. If you're going to run DEFRAG, do a little disk housekeeping first and delete all the outdated files that you don't need any more

To run DEFRAG, type **defrag** at the DOS prompt.

**WARNING**— It takes a while to optimize a big hard disk. It can take a couple of hours, so don't run DEFRAG until you have the time.

# DEL

Use DEL (or ERASE) to erase files.

## How to Enter It

**DEL filename**

## Examples

**DEL REPORT.DOC** erases the file named REPORT.DOC in the current directory.

**DEL C:\REPORTS\REPORT1.DOC** erases the file RE-PORT1.DOC in another directory.

**DEL A:\REPORT.DOC** erases the file named RE-PORT.DOC on a disk in drive A:.

**DEL *.DOC** erases everything ending in .DOC.

**DEL *.*** erases everything in the current directory (you'll be prompted about whether you really want to do this).

**DEL *.* /P** erases the directory file by file, prompting you whether you want each file erased.

> **TIP—** You can abbreviate DELETE as DEL but you can't shorten ERASE to ERA. DOS doesn't understand "DELETE," either. Use either DEL or ERASE. Very logical.

> **TIP—** Deleting everything in a directory doesn't delete the directory itself.

## Details

Deleted files aren't really removed from a disk; they're just marked as deleted, and DOS will eventually write over them. You can often get them back by using the UNDELETE command.

# DELOLDOS

Use DELOLDOS to delete the previous version of DOS (it's in a directory called OLD_DOS.*X*) and save yourself some disk space.

## How to Enter It

DELOLDOS

# DELTREE

Use DELTREE, new in DOS 6, to quickly clean off your disks by erasing entire directories and all the files and subdirectories in them, too.

## How to Enter It

**DELTREE directoryname**

## Example

Say that you want to delete your C:\WP51 directory and all its subdirectories—C:\WP51\DOCS, C:\WP51\MACROS, C:\WP51\LETTERS, C:\WP51\LETTERS\FEB, C:\WP51-\LETTERS\MAR, and so forth. Just entering **deltree c:\wp51** will delete them all. You don't have to delete the files in them first.

# DIR

## How to Enter It

**DIR** directory *options*

## Examples

**DIR** shows you the files that are in the current directory.

**DIR A: /P** shows the files that are in the current directory of the disk in drive A: and pauses after each screen is filled. To see the next screen of files, press a key on the keyboard.

**DIR /W** shows you a five-across list of the current directory's files. It leaves out most of the details and just shows file names.

**DIR *.DOC** lists all files ending in .DOC.

**DIR /O:N** alphabetizes the directory listing (/O:-N will alphabetize it in reverse order). In addition /O:E and /O-E will alphabetize it (or alphabetize it in reverse) by extension, /O:D and /O-D will sort it by date, and O/:S and O/:-S will sort it by size.

**DIR REPORT3.DOC** tells you whether the file RE-PORT3.DOC is in the current directory.

**DIR A: /A** displays only files that haven't been backed up. (The /A option lets you display files that have certain attributes; here, A represents the archive attribute. See ATTRIB for what the other attributes are.)

**DIR /S** lists the contents of all subdirectories.

**DIR /B** lists one file name per line, with no other information.

**DIR /L** lists names in lowercase.

**TIP**— *In the Shell, just highlight a directory name to see what's in it.*

**TIP**— *You can use wildcards with DIR.*

**TIP**— *To see if a file's in a directory without getting a whole directory listing, just type the file's name after DIR, like DIR OCT.RPT. If it's there, it will be listed. If it's not, you'll get a "File not found" or "Bad command or file name" message.*

**DIR /C**, new in DOS 6, displays information about the compression ratio on drives that have been compressed with DoubleSpace.

**TIP—** *Use DIR /P if you're looking in a directory with a lot of files in it. Otherwise, they'll just zip by.*

## Details

When you get a directory listing, you'll see the date and time the file was last modified or created and its size in bytes. You'll also get a report on how many files were located and the amount of free space (in bytes) on the disk.

If you use the /W option, you'll just see file names and the names of any subdirectories, plus the number of files and the amount of free space.

The notations . and .. at the beginning of a directory list are always there, even in an empty directory.

**TIP—** *To change to a different drive, type its letter followed by a colon, like A: to change to drive A.*

Use the TREE command if you want to see the directory structure itself.

To change to a different directory, use the CD command.

# DISKCOMP

Use DISKCOMP to compare two floppy disks.

## How to Enter It

> **DISKCOMP drive1 drive2** *options*

## Examples

**DISKCOMP A: B**: compares the floppy disk in drive A with the one in drive B.

**DISKCOMP A: A**: (or just DISKCOMP) compares two floppy disks, both in drive A. You'll be prompted to insert the second disk. Use this format if you have only one floppy drive of a given type.

> **TIP**— *It doesn't matter what order you put the disks in.*

## Details

Use DISKCOMP after you've done a DISKCOPY, to make sure that the copy was exact. If you user DISKCOMP after just copying files, the disks probably won't compare exactly, even though the copies are fine, because DOS will have put the files into different tracks on each disk.

There are two options, /1 and /8. /1 compares just one side of a double-sided disk, and 8 compares only 8 sectors per track on the disk. You'll probably never need to use these options.

DISKCOPY will only compare disks that have the same capacity.

# DISKCOPY

Use DISKCOPY to copy entire disks.

## How to Enter It

**DISKCOPY source target**

## Examples

**DISKCOPY A: B:** copies the disk that's in drive A onto a disk in drive B.

**DISKCOPY A: A:** (or just DISKCOPY) copies a disk onto another disk if you have only one floppy drive, or if you have one 5.25-inch drive and one 3.5-inch drive (you'll be prompted to insert the source and target disks as needed).

**DISKCOPY A: B: /V** verifies that the copy was correctly made.

> **TIP**— *In the Shell, choose Disk Copy from the Disk Utilities.*

## Details

The **source disk** is the one you're copying. The **target disk** (also called the **destination disk**) is the new copy.

You can't DISKCOPY a hard disk. Change to a floppy drive (either A: or B:) before using DISKCOPY.

DISKCOPY is the same (well, almost the same) as COPY *.*, which means "copy everything." For example, if you have a disk in drive A and you want to copy all the files that are on it (and there are no subdirectories) to a disk in drive B, you'd enter COPY *.* B:. OK, so when do you use DISKCOPY and

> **TIP**— *Label your source and target disks before you start so that you can tell them apart. It's easy to get mixed up halfway through copying!*

when do you use COPY? Well, with DISKCOPY, the source and target disks have to be the same size. You can't DISKCOPY a 5.25-inch disk onto a 3.5-inch disk. So here's where you'd use COPY (or XCOPY) instead. Or if you just want to copy a few files, not everything on the disk, you'd use COPY (or XCOPY *.* /S if there are subdirectories on the disk).

**TIP**— *You can use an unformatted disk as the target disk.*

# DOSKEY

DOSKEY starts a program that lets you recall DOS commands and create macros.

## How to Enter It

DOSKEY

## Details

Usually, when you give commands to DOS at the command line, you give them one at a time. Doskey lets you give several commands at once. It also tells DOS to remember what you did so that you can do it again without having to enter the commands from scratch. If you're a diehard command line fan, you'll love this feature.

Doskey isn't normally present when you start your computer. To put it in memory, type *doskey* at the command line. After it's loaded, you can type several commands at once, separating each with a Ctrl-T, which puts a paragraph mark (¶) on your screen.

Doskey keeps a list of all the commands you enter, and all you have to do is press F7 to see it. You can then choose which command you want to use again from this list by highlighting it and pressing Enter, or by pressing F9, typing the number of the command, and pressing Enter.

Doskey also lets you define macros. A macro is simply a set of instructions that you want to give to DOS. Defining macros is just slightly different from using Doskey the way you just did. Instead of separating commands with Ctrl-T, you use a dollar sign and T ($T).

Unfortunately, we don't have enough room to discuss everything Doskey can do here, as it's rather advanced.

# DOSSHELL

Use DOSSHELL to start the Shell, if it doesn't start automatically when you turn on your computer.

## How to Enter It

DOSSHELL

You can use the /T option to run the Shell in text mode, /G to run it in graphics mode, and /B to run it in black and white if you have a color monitor.

# EDIT

Use EDIT to start the Editor, which allows you to edit text-only (ASCII) files.

## How to Enter It

EDIT

## Details

The Editor, which was new in DOS 5, is a full-screen text editor. It's included in addition to the notorious DOS editor called EDLIN, which let you edit only line by line. (EDLIN is gone from DOS 6.) See the AUTOEXEC.BAT chapter for a peek at how to use the Editor.

**TIP—** *In the Shell, choose Editor from the Main group.*

# ERASE

See DEL; it's the same thing.

# EXIT

Use EXIT to return to the original command processor you were working with if you used the COMMAND command.

## How to Enter It

EXIT

If you started another version of DOS running (with COMMAND), EXIT lets you get back to the "original" DOS.

## Details

You'll sometimes type *exit* at the command line for other reasons. Some programs let you "exit to DOS" to carry out file management tasks like copying and formatting disks. To return to the program when you're through, type *exit*.

**TIP**— *If you exit temporarily from the Shell to the DOS prompt (with F3), you get back by typing* exit.

# EXPAND

Use EXPAND to expand a compressed file.

## How to Enter It

**EXPAND sourcefile targetfile**

## Examples

**EXPAND A:DOSSHELL.EX_ C:\DOS\DOSSHELL.EXE**
uncompresses the DOSSHELL.EX_ file and stores it in
your DOS directory on your hard disk.

**EXPAND A:*.EX_ C:\DOS** uncompresses all the compressed files that have an .EX_ extension on the disk in
drive A to your DOS directory on drive C.

## Details

DOS 5 and 6 come as compressed files. (A compressed file has
a _ as the last character in its extension.) Normally, Setup
uncompresses all these files when you install DOS. However,
if you ever need to expand just one or a few of these compressed files from the original setup disks, you can use the EX-
PAND command.

# FASTOPEN

Use FASTOPEN to let DOS keep track of where the files you most recently used are, so that it can find them again quickly.

## How to Enter It

**FASTOPEN drive:=number of files to keep track of**

## Examples

**FASTOPEN C:=100** tells DOS to keep track of the last 100 files you opened on drive C. (It will handle up to 999 files.)

**FASTOPEN C:** tells DOS to keep track of 34 files, the default.

**FASTOPEN C:=100 /X** tells DOS to use expanded memory, saving conventional memory for your programs.

## Details

This is a command that was very useful before DOS's SMARTDrive disk-caching program came along. If you use it, it should go in your CONFIG.SYS file. It speeds up disk access on a hard disk. You'd enter it in CONFIG.SYS like this:

INSTALL=C:\DOS

FASTOPEN.EXE C:=100

However, if you're using SMARTDrive in DOS 5 or 6, you don't need FASTOPEN, because SMARTDrive is a better alternative.

**WARNING—** *Don't run FASTOPEN from the Shell, or your computer may freeze up.*

# FC

Use FC to compare two files and display what their differences are.

## How to Enter It

FC file1 file2 *options*

## Examples

**FC C:OCT.RPT A:OCT.RPT** compares the two files and reports the lines that are different in them, followed by the first line that matches.

**FC C:OCT.RPT A:OCT.RPT /N** displays the line numbers.

## Details

It will zip by pretty fast on the screen, so press Ctrl-S to stop the display. Ctrl-C will stop it altogether.

FC assumes that you're comparing text files unless you give it one of the many rather exotic options (we won't go into them here) that tell it to compare binary (program) files, and so forth.

# FDISK

Use FDISK to create partitions on your hard disk (divide it into smaller "logical" disks).

## How to Enter It

FDISK

## Details

Typing FDISK starts a menu-driven program that lets you partition your hard disk, or divide it into two or more "logical" drives (drives that aren't physically separated but can be used as if they were. This is, believe it or not, logical to DOS). For example, I have an 200-Mb hard disk that's divided into two drives, C and D, mainly because my husband wants to use his own filing system and doesn't like mine. (Drive D is his.)

**WARNING—** *All data on your hard disk is destroyed when you use FDISK.*

Other people may want to run another operating system, such as UNIX, on their hard disk; partitioning the disk can let you have DOS on one drive and UNIX on another.

**TIP—** *First, create your partitions with FDISK. Then format the newly created drives.*

# FIND

Use FIND to locate a specific word or phrase in a group of files.

## How to Enter It

**FIND "word or phrase" *options* filenames**

## Examples

**FIND "Creative Solutions" LETTER1.DOC LET-TER2.DOC** searches the files LETTER1.DOC and LETTER2.DOC in the current directory for the phrase *Creative Solutions* and displays the lines containing the phrase.

**FIND "Brigette" /N C:\REPORTS\OCT.TXT NOV.TXT DEC.TXT** searches three files in the C:\RE-PORTS directory and displays the lines as well as the line numbers the name occurs on (the /N option does that for you).

**FIND "Brigette" /C C:\REPORTS\OCT.TXT** counts the number of lines that have the word or phrase.

**FIND "I said, ""Silence!"""" ACT1 ACT2 ACT3** searches the files for a phrase that uses quotation marks. Notice that you use two sets of quotation marks to do this.

**FIND /V "408)" CLIENTS** would search a phone list in a file named CLIENTS for all phone numbers that are *not* in the 408 area code (assuming the area codes are set up as (408) 555-1212). (The /V displays lines that *don't* contain the word or phrase you're looking for. You can use both /C and /V together to get the number of lines that don't have the matching pattern.)

**TIP—** *Use the /N option to display the line number of the lines that have a match.*

# Details

This is a handy command to use when you don't know the name of the file you're looking for, but you know that it's got a certain word in it—maybe the name of a company, or a personal name.

It matters whether you use uppercase or lowercase letters with this command; FIND will find *Ralph* if you enter "Ralph" but not if you enter "ralph". (Use the /I option to make the search not case-sensitive.) However, it perversely doesn't care about spaces; if you enter "book" it will find *book, books, bookman, bookish,* and so forth.

# FORMAT

Use FORMAT to prepare disks so that you can use them.

## How to Enter It

**FORMAT drive:** *options*

## Examples

**FORMAT A:** formats a disk in drive A.

**FORMAT A: /S** puts hidden system files on the disk so that it can be used as a startup disk. (If you have a hard disk, you'll probably never use this one except to make an emergency startup disk.)

**FORMAT A: /F:360** formats a disk in a high-capacity (1.2 Mb) 5.25-inch drive as a 360K disk. If you're planning to use the disk with a computer that has only a 360K drive, like an XT, do your formatting on the machine with the regular-capacity drive. The high-capacity drive will be able to read it just fine. Sometimes 360K disks formatted in high-capacity drives aren't readable when you get them in a regular-capacity drive.

**FORMAT B: /F:720** to format a 3.5-inch disk in a high-capacity (1.44 Mb) drive as a 720K disk so that it can be used in a 720K disk drive.

**FORMAT A: /Q** does a quick format on a disk in drive A that's been formatted before (you can't change the disk's formatted capacity with the /F option if you use this one). This is the same as a Quick Format in the Shell.

**FORMAT A: /U** does an "unconditional" format that won't let you use the UNFORMAT command on the disk (see UNFORMAT).

> **TIP**— *In the Shell, choose Format or Quick Format from the Disk Utilities.*

/1, /4, and /8 are options that let you format a disk as single sided (/1), format a 360K disk in a high-capacity (1.2 Mb) drive (/4), or format a 360K disk as 8 sectors per track (/8), used only with very old versions of DOS. You probably won't ever use any of these.

**TIP**— *There's also a /B option that just makes a bootable disk but doesn't put DOS on it.*

## Details

Formatting a disk destroys everything that's on it. Starting with DOS 5, if you haven't used the /U (unconditional) option, you can sometimes get the data back, though (see UN-FORMAT).

**TIP**— *Format disks for the smallest-capacity drive they'll be used with.*

After you format a disk, you'll be prompted for a label. You don't have to use one; you can just press Enter instead. Using a label can help you identify and organize your disks, though. You can use spaces in volume (disk) labels and use 11 characters, so they don't have to be as cryptic as file names.

**TIP**— *Don't use these characters in a disk label: + = / [ ] : ; , ? * \ < > |.*

After the formatting is done, you'll also see a whole lot of numbers that tell you how much space is available on the disk. This space is reported in bytes, which can be confusing. See the Disks chapter for some tricks to help you tell what's what.

DOS will also report if there are any bad sectors on the disk. If there are, you can probably use the disk for storing files, but don't use it for copying disks with DISKCOPY or for making important backup disks of programs.

**TIP**— *The advantage of quick formatting is that it lets you clear off all the files, directories, and subdirectories on a disk without having to repeatedly use DEL or DELTREE.*

# GRAPHICS

Use GRAPHICS if you want to print graphics screens.

## How to Enter It

**GRAPHICS printer** *options*

## Examples

**GRAPHICS** lets you print graphics screens on black-and-white printers.

**GRAPHICS COLOR4 /B** lets you print graphics screens on a color printer with an RGB ribbon, printing the background in color.

## Details

Normally you can print an image of what's on the screen (called a screen dump) by pressing Shift-PrtSc. However, graphics screens are a little different from normal text screens. If you're displaying graphic images, you won't be able to print them unless the GRAPHICS command has been issued.

To use GRAPHICS, you need to have a file named GRAPHICS.COM in the current directory. If it isn't there, give its path in the command (like C:\DOS\GRAPHICS).

If you print a lot of graphics screens regularly, put the GRAPHICS command in your AUTOEXEC.BAT file.

Oh, boy, there are a lot of options with this one. But you probably only have one printer, so you'll only use one of this impressive array: /B to print the background in color (on a color printer), or /LCD to print a liquid crystal display (like those used in some laptops), or /PRINTBOX:ID to select the

**TIP—** *You won't see graphics on your monitor unless you have a graphics display adapter in your system. If you do, your monitor will be called an EGA, VGA, PGA, or CGA (that G's for Graphics).*

size of the print box. For ID, enter either *std* (full size) or *lcd* (an exact-size screen from a liquid crystal display).

You can also use/R to print white on black (like what you see on the screen, but this eats up ribbon).

Get **help graphics** to see the switches used with a variety of different printers.

# HELP & FASTHELP

Use HELP to get help about DOS commands and FAST-HELP to get a quick list of them and what they do

## How to Enter It

**HELP command** or **command /?**

**FASTHELP**

## Details

Entering either HELP XCOPY or XCOPY /? gets you help on the XCOPY command.

Entering FASTHELP gets you a list of all the DOS 6 commands and a brief description of what each does.

# INTERLNK, INTERSVR

Use INTERSVR and INTERLNK to connect two computers from their parallel or serial ports so you can share files between them.

## How To Enter It

Put

**DEVICE=INTERLNK.EXE**

in your CONFIG.SYS file. Then, to link the computers (which must be connected via cable), use

**INTERSVR driveletter: driveletter:.**

To direct another drive from one computer to the other with INTERSVR running, use

**INTERLNK driveletter=driveletter.**

## Examples

To start INTRSVR, type INTRSVR followed by the drive letters of the drives on your computer, such as **INTERSVR C: A:** for a computer with one hard drive (drive C) and one floppy drive (drive A).

With INTERSVR running, to link drive D on one computer to drive E on another, use

INTERLNK D=E

For details about the many switches you can use, get **help intersvr** and **help interlnk**.

# JOIN

Use JOIN to fool DOS into thinking that two disk drives are actually one.

## How to Enter It

**JOIN drive: directory**

## Examples

**JOIN A: C:\SALES** joins drive A to the (empty) SALES directory on drive C, so you can use the files on both drives A and C as though they were all on drive C.

**TIP—** *You have to use an empty directory when you join a drive to it.*

**JOIN A: /D** removes the join so that drive A is treated as a separate drive again.

## Details

Why would you want to use JOIN? Well, it can save you some typing time if you're using a lot of files from the disk in drive A because you don't have to change to different drives and type long paths; you can just type the file names instead.

The directory you're joining the drive to must be at the root level, as in the example.

# KEYB

Use KEYB to select a different keyboard layout.

## How to Enter It

**KEYB key code, code page, filename**

(Key code is a two-letter code for the country (like FR for FRANCE); code page is the code page number of the character set you're using (see CHCP); and file name is the path to the keyboard definition file (KEYBOARD.SYS), which has all of the keyboard translation tables.)

**KEYB FR,850\DOS\KEYBOARD.SYS** loads the French keyboard translation table based on code page 850 (multinational) and tells DOS that the KEYBOARD.SYS file is in the DOS directory.

This is another one that you won't use very often. It's the last step in setting up your computer to work with other languages and different keyboard arrangements (the French use an AZ-ERTY keyboard instead of the QWERTY keyboard). See CHCP for an overview of what's involved.

Once you have set all this up, you can switch between your chosen foreign-language keyboard and the standard U.S. keyboard by pressing Ctrl-Alt-F1. Ctrl-Alt-F2 returns you to the foreign-language keyboard.

# LABEL

Use LABEL to create or change the volume label on a disk

## How to Enter it

**LABEL drive:label**

## Examples

**LABEL A:june sales** labels the disk in drive A as "june sales."

**LABEL** prompts you for the label you want to enter.

**LABEL A:** removes the disk label.

## Details

When your format a disk, you're asked if you want to use a volume label to help you keep track of what's on the disk. You can give the disk a name of up to 11 characters, including spaces (see FORMAT for the characters you can use). If you're not formatting a disk, you can use the LABEL command to change a disk's label or give it one, if it doesn't have one.

Once a disk has a label, you'll see it whenever you get a directory listing. You can also see what a disk's label is by using the VOL command.

# LOADFIX

Use LOADFIX to specify that a program run in the first area of conventional memory.

## How to Enter It

**LOADFIX programcommand**

## Example

**LOADFIX C:\PROGRAM.EXE** starts the program named PROGRAM and loads it into the first 64K of conventional memory.

## Details

You'll know you need to use LOADFIX if you get a "packed file corrupt" message when you try to start a program.

# LOADHIGH

Use LOADHIGH to load a program into upper memory (a special kind of memory on a 386 or 486 computer).

## How to Enter It

LOADHIGH program

## Details

Before you can use LOADHIGH (it can be abbreviated LH), you need to do a couple of things. First, you have to have a 386 or 486 computer. Then you have to put the lines

DEVICE = C:\DOS\EMM386.EXE

and

DOS = HIGH, UMB in your CONFIG.SYS file.

Once you've done that, you can load programs into the 384K or so of memory that's usually reserved for your video display and other things—whatever's left over after everything's running. Those are the mysterious UMBs—upper memory blocks. DOS itself will load into extended memory.

# MD (MKDIR)

Use the MD command to create a new subdirectory.

## How to Enter It

MD path directoryname

## Examples

**MD \SPREADS** creates a new subdirectory named SPREADS under your root directory.

**MD A:\SPREADS** creates a new subdirectory under the root directory on drive A.

## Details

If you want the new subdirectory under your current directory, you can omit the backslash. For example, if you were in a directory named LOTUS, you could create a SPREADS subdirectory by typing MD SPREADS.

> **TIP—** *In the Shell, choose Create Directory from the File menu.*

You can specify several different levels with the MD command. For example, MD C:\LOTUS\SPREADS\OCT\SALES will create the SALES subdirectory (you can only create one subdirectory at a time).

When you make a new directory, you don't automatically change to it. Use the CD command to change directories. It's a lot easier in the Shell.

To remove a directory, use the DELTREE command, new with DOS 6.

# MEM

Use MEM to see how much free memory you have.

## How to Enter It

MEM *options*

## Examples

**MEM** gives you a report of how much total memory you
have (in bytes), how many bytes of it are available, and
how much expanded and extended memory you have,
and **MEM /C** will show you how your programs are
using memory.

## Details

What's the difference between all these different kinds of
memory? DOS basically recognizes 640K of conventional
memory. However, if you have an 80286 computer (like an
IBM AT), you have 1 Mb of memory. That extra 384K of
memory is called expanded memory, and programs that were
developed specifically to use it, like Lotus 1-2-3, can use it. (If
you're wondering how this all adds up, it's because 1 Mb is
1024K.) Expanded memory is extra memory that you can
purchase and use with an expanded memory manager; it will
run even on 8086 and 8088 computers like an IBM XT. In
any case, DOS keeps on thinking that you have only 640K of
memory, because that's all it was designed to deal with.

Most 286 and higher computers come with more memory
than one megabyte, and that's all called extended memory.

There are a couple of exotic options you can use with MEM.
/PROGRAM displays which programs are in memory, and
/DEBUG displays detailed information about the programs
and memory usage.

# MEMMAKER

Use MEMMAKER to have DOS 6 optimize your system's memory usage.

## How to Enter It

MEMMAKER

## Examples

**MEMMAKER** optimizes memory usage by changing your AUTOEXEC.BAT and CONFIG.SYS files (and SYSTEM.INI, too, if you're running Windows) so that memory-resident programs take up less conventional memory, making it available for your programs to use.

**MEMMAKER /BATCH** lets you see what MEMMAKER is doing line by line.

**MEMMAKER /UNDO** undoes the changes MEMMAKER made.

## Details

With MEMMAKER, you don't have to figure out what's high memory and what's upper memory and which device drivers and programs can go where. A custom optimization option lets you specify what you want to put in upper memory (get **help memmaker**).

# MODE

Use the MODE command to see the status of the things you've connected to your computer, to reconfigure a printer for a different port, to select another display monitor, to adjust the keyboard's key repeat rate, to prepare your monitor and keyboard to use different character sets, and to redirect printer output from one port to another.

## How to Enter It

MODE

## Examples

**MODE CON** (an option new in DOS 4) shows you the status of your keyboard.

**MODE LPT1:=COM1:** redirects output from your first parallel printer ports (LPT1) to the first serial port (COM1).

## Details

Most of the time, you won't have to use this command. It's an advanced command that has many different uses. Unless you're involved in things like changing your video display from 25 lines by 80 columns to 43 lines by 80 columns, you'll never have, or want, to use it. If you do get the urge to use MODE, curl up with one of those doorstop-sized books.

# MORE

Use MORE to see files one screen at a time.

## How to Enter It

MORE < filename

## Example

**MORE < READ.ME** displays the contents of the
READ.ME file one screen at a time.

## Details

When you finish reading each screen, press any key on the keyboard to see the next screen.

The MORE command acts as a filter; that's why you have to
use the < symbol with it. If you forget to put that symbol in,
MORE will just echo back whatever you type at the keyboard
or show you a blank screen if you press Enter. Very annoying.
Press Ctrl-C to get out of this situation.

You can also view files one screen at a time with TYPE
READ.ME | MORE. (That's another special symbol called a
pipe.)

This is a useful way to read those "READ.ME" files that zip
past you on the screen too fast to read. MORE them instead
of TYPEing them.

If you try to read a program file (one that ends in .COM or
.EXE) with either MORE or TYPE, all you'll see is garbage.

**TIP**— *In the Shell, press
F9 to see what's in a
highlighted file.*

**TIP**— *MORE won't work
on disks that are write-
protected.*

# MOVE

Use MOVE, new in DOS 6, to move files and rename directories.

## How to Enter It

**MOVE path destination**

## Examples

To move a file name DOC.TXT in the current directory to the C:\DOCS directory, use **MOVE DOC.TXT C:\DOCS**. The DOC.TXT document in the current directory will disappear because it will be relocated to the C:\DOCS directory.

You can move a file and rename it at the same time. For example, to move a file named MEMO.TXT to the DOCS directory and rename it as MYDOC.TXT, do it this way:

> **MOVE MEMO.TXT C:\DOCS\MYDOC.TXT**

To move several files at once, separate their names with commas, like this:

> **MOVE MEMO1.TXT,MEMO2.TXT C:\DOCS**

To rename a directory, give the old name first and then the new name:

> **MOVE C:\oldname c:\newname**

> **WARNING—** You can only move directories at the same level in your filing structure, but you can move files to different levels.

# MSAV

Use MSAV to scan your computer for viruses when you tell it to.

## How to Enter It

```
MSAV
```

## Details

MSAV, new in DOS 6, scans your computer for known viruses when you issue the command. If you want virus protection to be on all the time, put the VSAVE command in your AUTOEXEC.BAT.

To scan a floppy disk in drive A, use **MSAV A:.**

# MSBACKUP

Use MSBACKUP in DOS 6 to back up and restore files.

## How to Enter It

MSBACKUP

## Details

MSBACKUP presents you with a series of screens you can make choices from, such as which files or directories to back up. See Chapter 8 for details and examples of using this utility, which is new with DOS 6.

# MSCDEX

Use MSCDEX, new in DOS 6, to access CD-ROM drives.

## How to Enter It

> **MSCDEX /D: driver**

## Details

Your CONFIG.SYS file must contain a DEVICE= or DEVICEHIGH= line that loads your CD-ROM driver before you can use MSCDEX, such as

**DEVICE=C:\CDROM.SYS /D:MSCD000.**

This statement loads the drive named CDROM.SYS (you would substitute the driver that came with your CD-ROM). The /D switch assigns it to the signature MSCD000.

You can have more than one CD-ROM drive as long as each one has one of these statements in your CONFIG.SYS file. The first driver will be MSCD000, the second will be MSCD001, and so forth.

In your AUTOEXEC.BAT file, put the MSCDEX command along with the driver signature and the letter of the drive you want your CD-ROM to be:

**C:\MSCDEX /D:MSCD000 /L:E**

The /L switch assigns the CD-ROM with the signature MSCD000 to drive E.

# MSD

Use MSD, new in DOS 6, to see an analysis of technical data about your computer system.

## How to Enter It

MSD

## Details

The MSD command examines your system and produces information about how much and what kind of memory you have, the video display you're using, your processor and its speed, the TSRs you're running, your disk drives and ports, and so forth.

If you need to call Microsoft Technical Support, you can print out the information that MSD provides so you can refer to it easily. To send it to the printer and create a file at the same time, give the command as

**MSD /P** *filename*

Where *filename* is the name you want to give the file that will contain the information, such as ANALYSIS.TXT.

# MULTICONFIG

Use the multiconfiguration commands INCLUDE, MENU-COLOR, MENUITEM, MENUDEFAULT, and SUB-MENU to set up different system configurations on the same computer.

# NLSFUNC

Use NLSFUNC to load support for different date, time, and currency formats for other countries and to enable you to switch among different character sets.

## How to Enter It

**NLSFUNC path to COUNTRY.SYS file**

## Example

**NLSFUNC C:\DOS\COUNTRY.SYS**

## Details

NLSFUNC (national language support) needs to know where a file named COUNTRY.SYS is. It contains all the different date and time format settings for various countries.

Normally you won't need to use this one, but if you want an overview of how it works with other commands, see CHCP.

# NUMLOCK

Use NUMLOCK in your CONFIG.SYS file to turn the Num Lock key off when you start your computer.

## How to Enter It

NUMLOCK OFF

## Details

At last, DOS 6 lets us turn off that Num Lock key. Many programs allow you to use the numeric keypad's keys as cursor movement keys when Num Lock is off. If you want to be able to enter numbers via the numeric keypad, just press the Num Lock key to turn it on.

# PATH

Use PATH to tell DOS which directories to search for program files, so that you don't have to change to the directory that contains a program before you can run it.

## How to Enter It

PATH drive:\directories; drive:\directories

TIP— Don't use any spaces in the path. DOS stops reading when it gets to a space.

## Examples

**PATH** displays the path to the directory where you are.

**PATH C:\;C:\DOS;C:\WP51** sets the search path as first, the root directory; then the DOS subdirectory; and then the WP51 subdirectory.

## Details

To add new programs to your path, use the Editor or your favorite word processing program in ASCII text mode (see the AUTOEXEC.BAT chapter for details). When you type the path, remember to use a semicolon to separate each path. Use a colon after your drive letter. Use a backslash between directories.

TIP— The PATH command is normally used in your AUTOEXEC.BAT file.

# POWER

Use POWER if you have a portable computer, to turn power management off and on.

## How to Enter It

**POWER** *options*

## Details

If you have a battery-operated computer, DOS 6's new POWER command allows you to conserve battery power by detecting when the computer is idle and reducing power consumption. Your CONFIG.SYS file must contain the line **DEVICE=C:\DOS\POWER.EXE** before you can use the POWER command.

For details on what your battery-powered computer can do, see its manual and then check out **help power**.

# PRINT

Use PRINT to print a text file (ASCII file) while you're doing other work.

## How to Enter It

**PRINT** *options* **filename**

## Examples

**PRINT LETTER2** prints LETTER2 (you'll be asked which device to use; just press Enter to use your first printer port).

**PRINT LETTER?** prints all files beginning with LETTER and ending in any one character (like LETTER2, LET-TER3, etc.).

**PRINT LETTER3 /C** cancels printing LETTER3 (the /C cancels printing the file you specify).

**PRINT /T** cancels all printing.

**PRINT** shows the status of the print queue.

> **TIP**— *In the Shell, type print at the command line and then choose Print from the File menu.*

## Details

The other options /B, /P, /Q /U, /S, and /M specify details like buffer size that you'll probably never use.

Most programs nowadays let you print while you're working on another document, so you may never have to use this command either. However, you can use PRINT to print on whatever printer is connected to your computer.

A neat use of the PRINT command is to let you print documents on a computer that doesn't have your word processing program on it. Suppose you've worked on a document in WordPerfect at home and you want to print it on a computer at work that doesn't have WordPerfect on it. You could take all your WordPerfect disks to work, install the program, and print your document, but using PRINT's a faster way. After you have your document formatted the way you want it, print it to disk. Printing to disk produces a formatted ASCII file that PRINT can recognize and use, and you can magically print the document from a computer that isn't running your word processing program.

Most word processing programs have a procedure that lets you do this, but you may have to dig it out of the manual, and it may be fairly complex. (Hint: in WordPerfect, with the document on screen, call up the Print menu, Select the printer the document's been formatted for, Edit it, select Port and Other, name the document with the name you'll use to print it—a .TXT extension will help you tell it from your other documents—exit back to the Print menu, and select Full Document. The document that's "printed" will be a disk file that you can take to another computer and print by using the PRINT command.)

See Chapter 9, "Printing," for more information about printing with DOS.

**TIP**— *You can't usually PRINT a file that you've created with your word processing program. It has all sorts of codes in it that DOS knows nothing about.*

**WARNING**— *Printing to disk isn't the same thing as saving to disk or printing from disk!*

**TIP**— *Another way to PRINT a file is to copy it to your printer (PRN), like this: COPY file PRN:.*

# PROMPT

Use PROMPT to change the DOS prompt (the A>, B>, C>).

## How to Enter It

**PROMPT** *options*

## Options

**$**   special character used with options

**-**   starts a new line

**b**   produces | (a bar)

**d**   produces the date

**e**   produces the Esc character

**h**   produces a backspace

**g**   produces > (greater than)

**l**   produces < (less than)

**n**   produces the current disk drive

**p**   produces the path

**q**   produces = (equals)

**t**   produces the time

**v**   produces the DOS version number

## Examples

**PROMPT $p$g** produces a prompt that shows you the current path to whatever directory you're in. (This is the most common use of PROMPT, and it's put in your AUTOEXEC.BAT file for you when you install DOS 5 and 6.)

**PROMPT $t** produces a prompt that shows the current time (as in 10:28:07.34).

**PROMPT $p&_You called, master?** displays the path, starts a new line, and presents the message "You called, master?".

## Details

Use the PROMPT command in your AUTOEXEC.BAT file to customize the system prompt however you like it. You might want to use your name instead of the "master" in the example.

To go back to the default prompt, C>, just type PROMPT at the prompt.

# QBASIC

Use QBASIC to start QBasic, a programming language utility that comes with DOS 5 and 6.

## How to Enter It

**QBASIC filename** *options*

## Examples

*QBASIC MYPROGRAM.BAS /EDITOR starts QBasic, opens the file MYPROG.BAS, and starts the DOS Editor.*

## Details

There are several options that control how you see in QBasic on your screen: /H displays as many lines of text as your monitor can; /B displays text in black and white, even if you have a color monitor; /NOHI lets you use a monitor that doesn't provide high-intensity video; and /G updates a CGA (color graphics) monitor as fast as possible. There's also a /MBF switch that makes QBasic treat IEEE-format numbers as Microsoft format numbers.

> **TIP**— *QBasic has online help. Just press F1 while you're in QBasic to get it.*

Teaching QBasic is more than we can do in this book, as you might have guessed.

# RD (RMDIR)

Use RD (or RMDIR) to remove an empty directory from your filing system.

## How to Enter It

RD directoryname

## Examples

**RD C:\DOCS\LETTERS** removes the subdirectory LETTERS.

## Details

Before you can delete a directory with RD, it has to be empty of everything except the two files represented by . and .. . It's much faster to use DOS 6's new DELTREE command.

# REN (RENAME)

Use REN (or RENAME) to give a file a new name.

## How to Enter It

**REN oldname newname**

## Examples

**REN LETTER1 LETTER2** renames the LETTER1 file as LETTER2.

**REN *.DOC *.TXT** renames all files ending in .DOC in the current directory to end in .TXT. LETTER1.DOC becomes LETTER1.TXT, LETTER2.DOC becomes LETTER2.TXT, and so forth.

**REN C:\DOCS\LETTER.DOC COMDEX.DOC** renames the file LETTER.DOC in the DOCS directory to be COMDEX.DOC. Note that you don't give a path with the new name.

**TIP**— *In the Shell, choose Rename from the File menu.*

## Details

Here's a command that really lets you put wildcards to work. You can rename big bunches of files at a time with wildcards in both the old names and the new names.

For example, suppose you wanted to rename a lot of files named SCREEN01, SCREEN02, SCREEN03, and so forth, as FIGURE01, FIGURE02, FIGURE03, and so forth. You could do that all with one command, as REN SCREEN?? FIGURE??. You could even change the extension at the same time. Say your SCREEN files had different extensions, like SCREEN01.CAP, SCREEN02.TIF, and so forth. Using REN SCREEN??.* FIGURE??.ART would give all those files an .ART extension.

**WARNING**— *Don't rename files with names that a program doesn't expect to find. WordStar looks for .WSD files, Lotus looks for .WKS files, and so forth.*

If you're trying to use wildcards to rename a bunch of files and keep getting the "Duplicate file name or File not found" message, there's already a file with (at least) one of those names in that directory. Figure out which one it is (get a directory listing) and rename that file TEMP; then rename the rest of the files; then rename the TEMP file to whatever you wanted it to be.

REN doesn't erase the original file; it's still there on disk, under its original name.

# REPLACE

Use REPLACE to update files with their newer versions.

## How to Enter It

**REPLACE file1 file2** *options*

## Examples

**REPLACE A:\*.TXT C:\DOCS /A** adds any new .TXT files that are on a floppy disk in drive A but not in the directory named DOCS on drive C to that directory. (The /A says "add files.")

**REPLACE A:\*.\* C:\ /S** searches all the subdirectories on drive C and replaces all the files that match the files on the disk on drive A. The /S says "replace files with the same names."

**REPLACE DOCS\MEMO LETTERS /U** replaces the MEMO document in the LETTERS directory with the MEMO document in the DOCS directory if it's a more recent version than the one that is already in the LETTERS directory. The /U says "replace just updated files."

## Details

This is a command that you probably won't use very often. It's mainly used when you get a disk with more recent versions of files that you already have on your hard disk. For example, you might get a set of updated printer drivers to use with a word processing program. Most software manufacturers usually supply an Update or Install program to automatically replace the old versions of the files with the new ones, though.

Note that you don't give the a file name, just a directory name, as the target; REPLACE searches for file names that match.

Use the /A option if you want to add files that are on the source disk (the new one) but not in the directory on your hard disk.

There are a couple of other options you can use: /P to be prompted before each file is replaced, /R to replace only read-only files, and /W to wait for you to insert a floppy disk.

# RESTORE

Use RESTORE to restore files that you've backed up with the BACKUP command in DOS versions earlier than DOS 6.

## How to Enter It

**RESTORE drive with backups destination drive**
*options*

## Examples

**RESTORE A: C: /S** restores all the backed-up files on a floppy disk in drive A onto the hard drive (C) back into their original subdirectories. The subdirectories will be created if they've been deleted. (The /S restores subdirectories.) The directory you backed up from should be your current directory on drive C; otherwise, give the directory name and the *.* specification for "all files."

**RESTORE A: C:\DOCS\*.* /P** restores files on a disk in drive A to the DOCS directory on drive C and prompts you if it finds a file on drive C that was changed after the backup. (The /P is for prompt.)

**RESTORE A: C: /M** restores only the files on the disk in drive A that have been modified since the last backup.

**TIP—** *You can't work with a backed-up file unless you've restored it to your hard disk.*

**RESTORE A: C: /A:02-16-93** restores only files that have been changed on or after February 16, 1993. Using /B:02-16-93 would restore only files that were changed before that date.

## Details

If you don't specify a destination, RESTORE restores files into your current directory. If that directory isn't the same one that you used when the files were backed up, you'll get a message saying no files were found to back up. You don't want that, so be sure to specify a destination and a *.* for "all files."

> **WARNING**— You can't change the name of a file when you restore it. Use the same name it was backed up under.

You can change the drive letter, though. For example, you can restore files backed up from C:\SPREADS to D:\SPREADS.

Be sure to restore files in the same order they were backed up. That's why you marked those disks as 01, 02, when you used the BACKUP command.

One other option, /N, restores files that aren't on the target disk any more (those that have been deleted since the last backup). This is handy to use if you're worried about restoring older files onto newer ones.

There are also time options that you can use.

/E:HH:MM:SS restores files that were modified on or before the specified time, and /L:HH:MM:SS restores files that were modified on or after that time. But be warned: using the time without a date can give you some very weird results!

If it's been a while since you made the backup, you may have edited some of the files on the hard disk, and they'll be a more recent version than the ones on the backup disks. If you think that might be the case, use the /P option so that you'll be prompted if DOS finds a more recent file on drive C.

With DOS 6, use MSBACKUP both to back up and restore files.

# SHARE

SHARE is used if you're working on a network to set up file sharing.

## How to Enter It

**SHARE** *options*

This one is best left to your network administrator. It sets up your system to allow file sharing.

Some program installation procedures don't like to SHARE. You may get strange messages. PageMaker won't recognize its own installation disks, for example. (Maybe they'll have fixed this by now, though.) To get around it, start your computer with a startup disk in drive A (see the FORMAT entry for how to do this).

# SMARTDRV

Use SMARTDRV to set up a disk cache, which speeds up most operations.

## Details

After you install DOS 6, you can run MEMMAKER, which optimizes your memory for you. One of the things MEM-MAKER does is set up a SMARTDrive disk cache and configure it for running both DOS and Windows.

If you want to change the values MEMMAKER selects or set up a SMARTDrive disk cache on your own, get **help smart-drv**.

# SORT

Use SORT to alphabetize lines in a file..

## How to Enter It

**SORT** *options*

## Examples

**SORT < CLIENT.DOC** sorts each line in the file CLIENT.DOC alphabetically and displays the results on the screen.

**SORT < CLIENT.DOC > PHONE.DOC** sorts each line in the CLIENT.DOC file alphabetically and puts the results in a file named PHONE.DOC.

**SORT /+25 < CLIENT.DOC** sorts the CLIENT.DOC file alphabetically beginning at position 25, so if last names began at that position (if the text were in regular columns), the file would be sorted by last name.

**SORT < CLIENT.DOC /R** does a reverse sort (one in which z is first).

## Details

SORT is one of those redirection commands that make you use the < and > symbols. If you leave out the <, your file won't get sorted.

SORT thinks numbers are characters and sorts them one by one. This can cause problems because it will sort as if 11 comes before 2. (Use leading zeroes like 02 to get around this.) It also doesn't recognize tabs, so if your file has tab spaces in it, the results may not be what you think.

**TIP**— *It's usually better to use a word processing program or database that has a sophisticated sorting routine, like WordPerfect or Microsoft Word, to sort files.*

# SUBST

Use SUBST to set up shorthand notation for long directory names.

## How to Enter It

**SUBST drive: path**

## Example

**SUBST E: C:\WORD\DOCS\LETTERS\JONES** lets you type E: instead of C:\WORD\DOCS\LETTERS\JONES to refer to the JONES subdirectory.

## Details

If you find yourself frequently having to type out long paths to a directory, you can set up a shorthand notation for them with SUBST. You can use drive D: or E: as a replacement for the long path names. (If you want to use other letters, you'll need to use the LASTDRIVE command in your CONFIG.SYS file to tell DOS what your last drive letter is, because it only knows about A through E.)

Like ASSIGN and JOIN, SUBST fools DOS into thinking one thing is actually another. Be careful not to use commands that require DOS to really know what's what, like RESTORE, while SUBST is in effect.

To remove a substitution, type SUBST followed by the substituted drive and a /D, as in SUBST E: /D for the example above.

To see what substitutions you've set up, type SUBST.

# SYS

Use SYS to make a disk that you can use for starting your system.

## How to Enter It

**SYS DRIVE:**

## Example

**SYS A:**

## Details

The SYS command puts hidden operating system files on a disk so that you can use it as a startup disk. If you have a laptop that runs from floppies, you may need to use this one from time to time.

Instead of using the SYS command, use FORMAT /S. It will format the disk, put the system files on it, and copy COMMAND.COM on it so that you don't forget to.

Normally you'll use SYS on a blank disk, but you can use a disk that already has files on it, assuming there's enough room on it for your system files.

# TIME

Use TIME to see the current time or to set the system time for the current session.

## Examples

**TIME**

displays the current time.

**TIME hh:mm:ss**

sets the time without prompting you.

**TIME 8:30p**

sets the time to AM/PM format.

## Details

You'll probably want to change the time at least twice a year for Daylight Savings time. But to set the time "permanently," you need to use a separate utility program (mine's called SET-CLOCK) that came with your system clock.

If you don't want to set the time, just press Enter after you're prompted for a new time.

If you don't have an AUTOEXEC.BAT file, you'll be prompted for the date and time each time you start your computer. Good reason to set one up if you don't have one already.

# TREE

Use TREE to get a graphic display of your file structure.

## How to Enter It

**TREE C:**

shows you the directories and subdirectories of the files on drive C:.

**TREE /F**

lists the files in the directories, too.

**TREE /A**

uses an alternate character set that's a little fancier than the regular one.

**TREE \**

shows you the directory structure starting at the root directory.

## Details

If you get lost in your filing system, you can use TREE to get an idea of how your directories are set up.

If you have a lot of directories, they will zip by pretty quickly. Use TREE | MORE to see long directory trees.

**TIP—** *If you just want to find a file somewhere in your subdirectories, use DIR /S. It's faster than TREE.*

# TYPE

Use TYPE to see the contents of a text file on the screen.

## How to Enter It

**TYPE filename**

## Examples

**TYPE READ.ME** shows the contents of a file named READ.ME in the current directory.

**TYPE READ.ME | MORE** displays the file one screen at a time.

## Details

When you buy a program, you'll often get a README file with it explaining last-minute changes and so forth. You can read these files before you start the program by using the TYPE command.

Use TYPE only with text files. If you use it on a program file (one that ends in .EXE or .COM), you'll just see garbage on the screen.

If the file is longer than one screen of text, use the MORE trick in the example above, or use the command as MORE < READ.ME.

**TIP—** *In the Shell, press F9 to see what's in a highlighted file.*

**TIP—** *You can also use Ctrl-S to stop scrolling and Ctrl-Q to start it again.*

# UNDELETE

Use UNDELETE to get deleted files back.

## How to Enter It

**UNDELETE filename option**

## Examples

**UNDELETE /S** (in your AUTOEXEC.BAT file) sets up Delete Sentry protection in DOS 6.

**UNDELETE /T** (in your AUTOEXEC.BAT file) sets up Delete Tracker protection in DOS 6.

**UNDELETE** recovers all deleted files in the current directory one at a time.

**UNDELETE C:\\*.DOCS /ALL** undeletes all files in the root directory of drive C that end in .DOC.

**UNDELETE /LIST** lists the files that can be undeleted.

**UNDELETE /ALL** recovers all deleted files without prompting you.

**UNDELETE A:OLDFILE** undeletes the file named OLDFILE on the disk in drive A.

## Details

When you install DOS 6, you'll be asked whether you want to install deletion protection for DOS, Windows, or both. Once it's installed, you can decide whether you want to use either Delete Sentry or Delete Tracker (see Chapter 10 for how to put this protection in your AUTOEXEC.BAT file). Delete Sentry creates a hidden directory named C:\SENTRY that

**WARNING**— *Undelete can't recover deleted directories. And it can't recover a file if you deleted the directory that contained it. Windows Undelete may be able to recover a directory, though.*

holds all the files you delete. When you delete a file, it's simply moved to the C:\SENTRY directory.

With Delete Tracker, only the names and locations of files you delete are saved. If you haven't specified either method of deletion tracking, you can still undelete files, if you try to get them back right away, before they're overwritten by other files you may have saved later.

When you type **undelete** and press Enter, DOS 6 assumes you want to use Delete Sentry, if it's available, or Delete Tracker, if it's available. If you haven't set up either one of these, DOS 6 will still sometimes let you undelete files that haven't been overwritten. If DOS reports that the MS-DOS directory contains any deleted files that can be recovered, type **undelete /dos** at the command prompt and press Enter. You'll be prompted for the first character in each file's name; just enter any character, and DOS will undelete the file.

# UNFORMAT

Use UNFORMAT to restore a disk that you've formatted by mistake.

## How to Enter It

UNFORMAT drive *options*

## Examples

**UNFORMAT A:** unformats the disk in drive A.

**UNFORMAT A: /TEST** or **UNFORMAT A: /J** test to see whether the disk in drive A can be unformatted.

**UNFORMAT A: /P** gives you a printed copy of the UNFORMAT process (turn your printer on first!).

## Details

This handy command restores a disk to the way it was before you formatted it. If you need to use it on a hard disk, you'll have to start your system from a floppy disk in drive A. That disk should have a CONFIG.SYS file on it so that DOS can tell what devices you're using. The Uninstall disk created when you installed DOS 6 will do.

**WARNING**— You can't unformat a disk that's been unconditionally formatted (with FORMAT /U).

# VER

Use VER to see the version number of DOS you're using.

## How to Enter It

VER

## Details

Why would you need to know this? Well, you might be at somebody else's computer and not know which version of DOS was on it. Each new version of DOS has commands that previous versions don't have.

# VERIFY

Use VERIFY to make sure that files are written on the disk correctly, especially when you're making copies.

## How to Enter It

**VERIFY ON, VERIFY OFF**

## Details

If VERIFY is on, all disk writing operations, like saving a file, will be double-checked automatically. You may want to put VERIFY ON in your AUTOEXEC.BAT file, but it does slow down your hard disk a little.

You can also use COPY or XCOPY with the /V option instead of turning VERIFY on.

> **TIP—** *The shorthand for VERIFY is not VER. That's a different command. There's no shorthand for VERIFY.*

# VOL

Use VOL to see the volume label on a disk.

## How to Enter It

VOL driveletter

## Example

**VOL A:** shows the volume label of the disk in drive A.

## Details

If you've used the LABEL command to make a disk label, you can see what that label is by using VOL, or see that there's no label at all on the disk, which is perfectly OK, too. Using volume labels is completely optional.

You'll also see a volume serial number, which I've never found any good use for. Maybe if you have, you could write me and tell me, along with who wrote that great line that opens this chapter.

# VSAFE

Use VSAFE to have DOS 6 constantly monitor your system for viruses.

## How to Enter It

**VSAFE** *options*

## Options

1    Checks for viruses that can destroy your hard disk.

4    Checks executable files for viruses.

5    Checks boot sectors of all disks for anything that tries to write to them.

6    Checks for anything that tries to write to the boot sector of your hard disk.

8    Checks for anything that tries to modify executable files.

There are three more options you can use:

2    Checks for anything that attempts to stay in memory.

3    Checks for anything that tries to write to disk.

7    Checks for anything that tries to write to a floppy's boot sector.

## Details

Put VSAFE and any of its options in your AUTOEXEC.BAT file so that virus protection will always be on when your computer's running.

# X-COPY

Use XCOPY for copying files or whole directories and sub-directories.

## How to Enter It

**XCOPY source file**

or

**directory target file**

or

**directory** *options*

## Examples

**XCOPY C:\DOCS A:** copies all the files in the DOCS directory onto a disk in drive A. Adding a /V after the A: verifies each copy.

**XCOPY C:\DOCS A: /S /E** copies all the files in the DOCS directory, plus any subdirectories that may be under it, even if they are empty, to a disk in drive A. (/S copies all subdirectories of the directory you specify, but not empty subdirectories, and /E copies even empty subdirectories, preserving the original structure.)

**XCOPY C:\DOCS A: /P** prompts you before each copy is made.

**XCOPY A: C:\REPORTS** copies all the files on the disk in drive A to a directory named REPORTS on drive C. If the REPORTS directory doesn't exist, XCOPY creates it at the root directory.

**XCOPY C:\DOCS A: d:02-16-93** copies only files that have been changed on or after February 16, 1993.

**TIP—** *Notice that you put your options after the target.*

**XCOPY C:\DOCS A: /S /A** is a little trickier. This is a good way to make an incremental backup without using DOS 6's backup utility—only files that you've worked with will be copied. The /A copies only files that have been changed since the last time you used XCOPY with the /M option (see below).

**XCOPY C:\DOCS A: /S /M** is even more tricky. It tells DOS to copy the files in the DOCS directory and its subdirectories that have been changed (modified), but also to tag the file with an archive attribute so that it won't be copied the next time unless the file's been changed. Practically speaking, this means that you can use XCOPY to keep your files up to date (see Details).

## Details

XCOPY gives you a couple of advantages over COPY. For one thing, it lets you preserve your directory structure if you use the /S option to copy entire subdirectories and the /E option to copy them even if they don't have any files in them.

> **TIP**— You can use wildcards with XCOPY.

So when should you use XCOPY? Well, just about any time you'd use COPY. XCOPY's a little faster. Also, if you're copying whole directories and their subdirectories, XCOPY is the best choice.

Use DOS 6's MSBACKUP if you're backing up your hard disk or entire directories onto floppy disks. It's a big improvement over the BACKUP command found in earlier versions of DOS. See Chapter 8 for details about MSBACKUP.

> **WARNING**— You can't use unformatted disks with XCOPY. Have a supply of formatted disks on hand before you begin.

The bottom line? If you work with only a few files each day, you'll find XCOPY easy to use to make copies of your daily work. First, put your backup disk in drive A; then, for example, if you've worked in the \WP51 directory, you'd give the command as XCOPY C:\WP51 A: /S /M. Only the files you've worked with since the last time you used XCOPY will be copied.

# Appendix:
# Installing DOS 6

DOS 6 comes with a special installation program called Setup. You need to use it to upgrade to DOS 6; you can't just copy what's on the installation disks onto your hard disk, because what's on those disks is in a compressed format.

The Setup program will automatically check to see what kind of hardware you have and will ask you to verify what it finds.

To use the Setup program, if your computer's running and you already have a version of DOS on it, put Disk 1 in drive A (or B) and close the drive door. Type *A:* (or *B:*) and press Enter to make that drive current. Then type *setup* and press Enter. You'll see instructions on the screen for each step to take, and you can press F1 to get online help.

Early in the Setup program, you'll be asked to provide either two regular-density floppy disks or one high-density floppy disk that's compatible with your drive A. They don't have to be formatted. You'll be asked to label them "Uninstall 1" and "Uninstall 2."

> **WARNING**— *Before you install DOS 6, turn off anything that may try to give you an automatic message while you're installing, such as a network message service.*

> **TIP**— *If you're running OS/2, read the file OS2.TXT on Disk 1 before you install DOS 6. If you're on a network, read NET-WORKS.TXT on Disk 1. There's also a very useful README.TXT file, which Setup will refer you to if you encounter problems.*

## Installing Anti-Virus, Backup, and Undelete

DOS 6 comes with three new, improved utility programs—Microsoft Anti-Virus, Backup, and Undelete—in both DOS and Windows versions. Watch the on-screen instructions carefully so you can decide whether you want just the Windows version, the DOS version, or both. I recommend both. If you install the Windows versions, Setup creates icons for them as well as a new Microsoft Tools group in the Program Manager.

If you don't have room for both versions of these programs (you'll need about 7 Mb of free space, total, for all that DOS

> **TIP**— *After you've installed DOS 6, be sure to make backup copies of your DOS disks as soon as possible, by using the Disk Copy utility or the DISKCOPY command. See Chapter 8 for details.*

6 has to offer), you can add them later, after you've installed DOS 6 and after you've run its disk compression program to free space on your hard disk. Put Setup Disk 1 in drive A (or B) and at the command line type *a:setup /e* or *b:setup /e*. Then follow the on-screen instructions.

## Using DoubleSpace

When you've finished installing DOS 6, you can compress your hard disk. My advice is to do it; although the process takes a while, you'll wind up with a faster hard disk with much more room on it. You won't be able to uninstall DOS 6 if you run DoubleSpace, though, so you may want to wait a few days until you're comfortable with DOS 6 before you compress your disk. I installed it immediately and was *very* happy with it, though: I went from 3 Mb of free space to 85 Mb of free space! To run DoubleSpace, type *dblspace* at the command prompt and follow the instructions on the screen. When it starts to defragment your hard disk (you'll see a chart on the screen showing what it's doing to your disk), go away. Get coffee. Go shopping. On a big hard disk, this will run for about an hour or more.

## Using MemMaker

When you've finished installing DOS 6, you can also let DOS 6 optimize your memory usage by running a new Mem-Maker utility that analyzes your system and sets up your AU-TOEXEC.BAT and CONFIG.SYS files for you. My advice again is to let DOS do the work for you—run MemMaker and let it configure your memory instead of dealing with it yourself. This time, stay there. DOS will show you error messages as MemMaker works, if there are any problems, and you'll need to know about these. It will restart your computer a couple of times. Just sit there and watch the screen. Keep your hands off the keyboard until MemMaker asks you whether you saw any error messages. To run MemMaker, type *memmaker* at the command prompt.

## Details

Even if you don't run MemMaker (which is only for 386 and higher computers), the Setup program will change lines in your AUTOEXEC.BAT and CONFIG.SYS files so that DOS 6 will work properly. It will create new AUTOEXEC.BAT and CONFIG.SYS files and rename your old ones so that you can get them back later, if you need to.

Setup will also keep your old version of DOS and save it in a directory named OLD_DOS.1. You can use the Uninstall disk that was created during setup to return to this version of DOS if you ever have to, or just delete your old DOS directory by typing **deloldos** at the command prompt. You can also use this Uninstall disk as an emergency startup disk in case something happens to your hard disk. To start your computer with it, put the Uninstall 1 disk in drive A and turn on your computer (or press Ctrl-Alt-Del to restart it).

> **TIP**— *See the AUTOEXEC.BAT and CONFIG.SYS chapter (Chapter 10) if you need more information about what these special startup files do.*

## Oh, No! A Disk Error!

You may get a disk error message while Setup uncompresses files and copies them onto your hard disk. This can happen if there's a bad spot on your hard disk or one of your floppy disks. If this happens, try running Setup again.

If all the files except just a couple get uncompressed and copied, here's how to uncompress them manually and get them onto your hard disk (this happened to me with DOSSHELL, which is a very important file).

You can tell which files are compressed on the floppies; they're identified by a _ at the end of their name. For example, DOSSHELL.EX_ identifies the compressed DOSSHELL file. There's a utility (which thankfully is *not* compressed) called EXPAND.EXE that will let you set these compressed files free. It's on Disk 1.

Once EXPAND.EXE is on your hard disk, you can expand a compressed file that's on a disk in drive A like this:

    EXPAND A:DOSSHELL.EX_
    C:\DOS\DOSSHELL.EXE

Just remember to give the whole name (.EXE or whatever) at the end, in place of the _.

## Oh, No! It Won't Start!

If your computer won't start from your hard disk after you've installed DOS 6, you can try this procedure. DOS 6 lets you start "interactively"—that is, by running each command in your AUTOEXEC.BAT and CONFIG.SYS files line by line. Restart your computer by pressing Ctrl+Alt+Del. When you see the message "Starting MS-DOS..." press F8.

> **WARNING**— *Once you've installed DOS 6, don't start your computer with a startup floppy disk from a previous version of DOS. Use the Uninstall disk or Setup Disk 1 instead.*

You'll be prompted for each line that's in your CONFIG.SYS. Press Y for all of them, but when you're asked about the device named EMM386.EXE, press N. When you're asked whether to run AUTOEXEC.BAT, press Y. If your computer doesn't start, the problem may be with the EMM386 memory manager. Type **memmaker** at the command line, let Mem-Maker optimize memory, and see if that fixes the problem.

If it doesn't, you have some more testing to do. Restart your computer, but this time, press F5 at the "Starting" message. DOS will start without running your AUTOEXEC.BAT or checking your CONFIG.SYS files. If your computer starts, it's one or the other of these files that's causing the problem. Call Microsoft! The number is 206/646-5104. You get 90 days' free support with DOS 6; why not use it?

> **WARNING**— *If you forget and leave the Uninstall disk in drive A after you've installed DOS 6, your computer will automatically run the Uninstall program when it starts and you'll be asked whether you want to go back to a previous version of DOS. (If you do, you'll have to install DOS 6 again.) Just type e to Exit.*

## *Oh, No! It Won't Install!*

If you can't get Setup to work for you, here's the brute-force way to install DOS 6. It involves making a startup disk that will jump-start your computer from drive A. Usually the situation is that you got DOS 6 on 3.5-inch disks and your drive A is a 5.25-inch drive. Most of the time, starting from drive A will give you access to the Setup program, but if it doesn't, you can install DOS 6 manually, and I'll tell you how to do that, too.

To make a startup disk for drive A, exit from the Setup program. Put Setup Disk 1 into drive A or B and put a blank floppy into drive A. At the command prompt, type *a:setup /f* (if Disk 1 is in drive A) or *b:setup /f* (if Disk 1 is in drive B). Then just follow the instructions on the screen.

When your startup disk is made, restart your computer by putting the disk in drive A and then pressing Ctrl-Alt-Del. Now you should be able to use the Setup program, delete files from your hard disk to make room for DOS 6, or do anything else you need to before installing.

If you still can't install DOS 6, try installing it manually, this way. You'll need a startup disk that's compatible with drive A (see the preceding instructions). Start your computer with that disk in drive A (press Ctrl-Alt-Del). Then transfer the system files to your hard disk by typing this at the command prompt: *sys a: c:* and pressing Enter. After that, type *a: setup /q* and press Enter. Follow the instructions on the screen. This will put the DOS system files on your hard drive and copy the DOS files directly to it.

Finally! Take the disk out of drive A and restart your computer. If this doesn't work, call Microsoft Technical Support for some more hints about what may be going wrong.

## Oh, No! I've got a PS/1!

If you've got a PS/1 and you can't install DOS 6, you've got a different procedure to follow. Turn your computer off. Then hold both mouse buttons down and turn the power on again. Choose  the Your Software icon from the System menu. Click on the DOS folder and double-click on CUSTOMIZ. In the How System Starts screen, choose Try Diskette First, Then Try Fixed Disk. Then select Read CONFIG.SYS and From Disk, and Read AUTOEXEC.BAT and From Disk. Press Enter to save the changes and restart with Ctrl-Alt-Del. Now you should be able to install DOS 6.

# Index

# We'd like to hear from you!

**Copy and mail or fax this page back to us for more information about other Peachpit books.**

## I'd like to know more about Peachpit's:

☐ DOS books

☐ Windows books

☐ Books on other topics (specify):

_____

_____

☐ Quantity discounts for (circle):
Dealers or school trainers
Corporate government user groups

Please tell us what you think of this book:

_____

_____

_____

_____

_____

_____

Name

Organization

Address

City/State/Zip

☐ Check here if you'd rather not receive computer-related information from other companies.

**Peachpit Press, Inc.**
2414 Sixth Street
Berkeley, CA 94710
Phone: 510/548-4393 ▼ 800/283-9444
Fax: 510/548-5991